BRENT
Never Forgets

I am not an elephant, and neither are you. As humans, we tend to forget things. When we forget to do what we COULD HAVE and SHOULD HAVE done to a client, we cause brand damage. When we forget to do what we COULD HAVE and SHOULD HAVE done to a prospect, we have unconverted leads and lost opportunities.

Let this book and the companion toy elephant (along with your well-appointed CRM, Marketing Automation & Sales Automation platform) be the B.R.E.N.T. (Business Relationship System for your ENTERPRISE).

BRENT Never forgets, and with Brent on your desk, neither will you.

For Dentists Only

A BUSINESS OWNER'S GUIDE TO SETTING UP INTEGRATED, AUTOMATED MARKETING

BRENT
Never Forgets

How to attract, nurture, and convert leads into life-long customers with BRENT's automated sales and marketing system

PARTHIV SHAH

Parthiv Shah., author

BRENT Never Forgets
How to attract, nurture, and convert leads into life-long customers with BRENT"s automated sales and marketing system / Parthiv Shah.

ISBN 9780990505969

Welcome and Thank You!

Thank you for investing in a copy of my book. I appreciate your support and would like to give you access to a guide I created "Business Kamasutra, From Persuasion To Pleasure, The Art of Data and Business Relationships". This valuable guide gives you specific tactics to turn your business acquaintances into lifelong, prosperous relationships. It includes strategies on:

- Segmentation (chapter 3)
- Project planning (pages 42-56)
- Atomization (58-67)
- Outsourcing (page 74)
- Combining technology and training to grow your business (78-91)
- And much more!

Click here to Access Business Kamasutra;

https://BusinessKamasutra.com

From Persuasion To Pleasure, The Art of Data and Business Relationships

Also by Parthiv Shah

- *The Iceberg You Don't See: The Marketing System for Financial Advisors*

- *Business Kamasutra: The Art of Data and Business Relations*

- *Business Kamasutra for Attorneys*

- *Business Kamasutra for Dentists*

- *Business Kamasutra for Pain Management Clinics*

- *"Ask": What Every Business Needs to Know About Making Money Predictably*

- *Pixel Estate: How to Attract, Nurture, and Grow Leads by Building Web Pages That Sell*

- *Secrets of the World's Most Potent & Persuasive Marketing Messages*

A BUSINESS OWNER'S GUIDE TO SETTING UP INTEGRATED, AUTOMATED MARKETING

Forword:
"Stop This Insanity!"
by Dan S. Kennedy

There is a famous house in San Francisco, where rooms kept getting added on, randomly, in response to some need or impulse. It grew as if constructed by drunks or lunatics. There are even stareways to nowhere. **This is the crazy way most small to mid-sized businesses' marketing "system" gets built.** Things added on, here and there, now and then, NOT integrated, in response to some new "tech" or software sold to them or some new online media that seems to require presence and content. It is a mess. It is frustrating. It wastes countless opportunities, with leads, prospects; customers, clients or patients.

The *feeding* of the business — new customer acquisition, retention, full monetization, and referral value — is, *therefore*, inconsistent, unreliable, has surges and slumps (sometimes inexplicable and mysterious), and creates vulnerability and fragility. The great investor Warren Buffet says "You never know who's naked until the tide goes out." The term of the China Virus and its disruption to so many businesses and business norms was a tide that went out and stayed out, exposing all sorts of nudity; of vulnerability, fragility. It also revealed some businesses with surprising strength. The system-deficient businesses doing marketing as a verb, and as random and erratic acts, drowned. Competition comes to challenge. For a time, the arrival of a Wal-Mart in a town sent many local businesses looking for tall ledges to leap from. More recently it has been Amazon striking terror in hearts. But the uncomfortable truth is that most businesses that are vulnerable to harm from the outside are vulnerable because of severe, "papered over" weaknesses inside.

If your business contains a "marketing house" like the one in San Francisco, with rooms added on and even stairways to nowhere… **You can STOP THIS INSANITY.**

If, at times, this mess in your business drives you crazy, you are right to be frustrated and angry, to feel impotent, and to be worried. If, at times, you think: this "thing" should be "easier" by now, you're likely right.

This insanity; chaos; inefficiency, and this fragility, vulnerability, and uncertainty can all be replaced with one fully integrated, largely "set it and forget it" automatic and automated marketing machine. Architected and engineered from the ground up, with clarity, and for consistency. It even converts "marketing" from something you *do* to a collection of *assets you own*, that work for you, in perfectly orchestrated concert.

This remarkable book, about BRENT, explains, in *full* detail, *exactly* how this is done. Importantly, there is NO "theory" here. This is NOT a whiteboard presentation by some professor of marketing at a university, who would put a Dairy Queen® into bankruptcy in a month if plucked from his comfy classroom to run it. I have known and worked with the author of this book, Parthiv Shah, for many years, and know him to be "for real" on this, the assembly of a TRUE "system" and "machine," tweaked for any business, from a thoroughly proven set of blueprints, with a thoroughly proven box of tools. *When he installs this in a business, its owner can actually relax,* liberated from repetitive stresses to, instead, create, innovate, expand or/and "play more golf" — whatever your "golf" is.

I will warn you: this book is _NO_ FUN. It is *not* "light" reading, mostly because it is not about lofty ideas. Because it is about very detailed, in-depth system construction. This will require *seriousness* on your part. One important thing to do as you proceed is to keep comparing what Parthiv is describing with what you now have, in your business. Challenging yourself in this way isn't any fun either. When you ask the mirror who's the smartest of them all, you want to say: you. But one of the most universal and neglected types of thinking required by success is NOT "positive" thinking, but, as Napoleon Hill characterized it, *"accurate"* thinking. Without it, you 're stuck. So, this book is going to require some serious, challenging thinking from you. It WILL be worth it.

DAN S. KENNEDY is a multi-millionaire serial entrepreneur, investor, and direct marketing strategy consultant to businesses from $1-million to $1-billion. He is the author of the popular NO B.S. book series including *No B.S. Guide to Ruthless Management of People & Profits* and *No B.S. Guide to Marketing to the Affluent.* His most recent business book is *Almost Alchemy: More from Fewer and Less.*

Contents

Forward

PART 1
Welcome

PART 2
Blueprint for Brent's
Automated Sales & Marketing System

PART 4
The Journey Forward

PART 1

Hi, I am **BRENT**
eLaunchers
eLaunchers.com

Welcome

"Marketing today is less about the sale and more about the journey."

— John Jantsch,
Duct Tape Marketing

WHO SHOULD READ THIS BOOK?

No one knows more than I do how little time you have as an entrepreneur or business owner. That's why if my book is not for you, I don't want to waste what little time you do have reading it. So I'm going to be crystal clear about who can benefit from reading this.

I wrote this book for entrepreneurs and business owners who want to understand the components and phases of sales and marketing automation systems and their technology. The acronyms and terms marketers and tech gurus throw around can confuse and frustrate the best of us, and I will define each of them before explaining how they work and why they are essential. Most of all, I want you to see why these sales, marketing, and technology components are necessary and how they fit together.

This book is for local business owners, business executives, service people, and online entrepreneurs with one question in common. "How do I attract, capture, and build connections with my potential customers that convert into lifelong revenue-producing relationships?"

What I'm about to share in this book will show you a step-by-step process of how you can do precisely that.

If you can take the knowledge and expertise you have of your current customer relationships and apply it to the BRENT system, which I will define a little later in this book; then I wrote this book for you.

This Book Is For The Person Who Will:

- Take an honest look at where their business systems are succeeding and failing

- Admit that they may not have or know what an effective business marketing and sales system is or if they do have one, realizing it is not working well

- Accept information and feedback on what is working and what is not working with their current sales, marketing, and technology system

- Admit they have little or limited knowledge of sales and marketing systems

- Confess to a certain confusion over the thousands of technology systems designed for supporting business automation

- Acknowledge their customer relationship management system may be letting customers slip through the cracks

- Own up to confusion over how the sales funnels work with their business system

- Accept they have a lot to learn about attracting, maintaining, and wowing their new and existing customers

- Disclose their absence of knowledge over where customers are positioned on their sales pyramid

- Feel a need for a system that incorporates sales, marketing, and technological automation to free them up to focus on building their business rather than working in i

This Book Is For The Person Who Will Focus On:

- Applying an efficient system that quickly increases the speed of sales

- Adopting a system that automates and streamlines business processes and efficiencies

- Implementing marketing architecture that builds lifelong customer relationships

- Offering helpful content to prospects first and then connecting the dots to their products or services

- Enabling themselves to complete this book in about an hour

- Making money through nurturing prospects to take the next steps in their buyer's journey

- Leveraging technology to automate the majority of their sales funnel processes

- Learning how to turn leads into customers through a well-organized and planned sales funnel

- Applying direct marketing and shock and awe packages to their sales strategy

- Understanding the value of a content management system

- Realizing the potential of a customer relationship management system

- Leveraging an all-in-one sales and marketing strategy, everything together in one place

Have no doubt; I'm going to share with you how you can achieve greater profits by integrating automated, personalized, high conversion marketing campaigns that build lifelong customers.

If that sounds like something you'd like for your business, please keep reading…

MY PROMISE
TO YOU

If you're still reading, I promise not to waste the next approximately one hour of your life. I sincerely hope you take the information this book gives you and take the follow up steps to move your business forward.

Those who know me appreciate that I take my responsibility to the entrepreneurial community seriously and volunteer my time by helping fellow entrepreneurs with pro bono marketing consulting to emerging entrepreneurs seeking assistance from seasoned, experienced mature organizations. They also know I am a respected teacher of marketing and e-business with a reputation for excellence backed by experience.

I promise to lend a hand to give you a proven and effective strategy for marketing with state-of-the-art technologies to execute your sales automation. Through automation, you will position yourself as the authority to build the know, like, and trust factor with your customers for your product or service. I'm going to tell you everything I know to make sure you have everything you need. In exchange, you need to put in some effort as well. Take the responsibility to read this book and consider my information with an objective mindset.

In February 2002, when I left the J M Perrone Company to start ListLaunchers, we had a prayer ceremony at our new offices. Sitting on the floor, in front of my family, friends, and business associates, the priest said the following prayer. I still remember every word of it, as if it were yesterday:

"You have now embarked on a new journey by starting this business. For the next 1000 days, we the family, we the religion, we the society, relieve you of all your earthly responsibilities. Now, this is your place of work. This is your place of worship; this is your home, this is your playground. Sit down, get to work, and for the next 1000 days, commit your heart and soul to focus on making this work. At the end of 1000 days, you will be a successful businessman, a better family man, a better religious man, and a philanthropist who will be committed to making the world a better place!"

I want to start this book by saying this prayer for all my fellow entrepreneurs. May God bring you the same success he has brought to my family and me!

It is my heartfelt opinion that what I'm about to share is:

- The most effective long-term way to connect with potential customers

- The most intelligent sales, marketing, and technology strategy to promote your business or service

- The fastest way for to build a successful business

- The simplest, most straightforward way to capture, nurture and develop leads into lifelong customers

Needless to say, if you need or want more details outside of what I was able to cover in this book, you can reach out to me or access my other books, success blueprint, and CD by visiting www.elaunchers.com.

Introduction

There are a few things I want to tell you about me before I start. Firstly, I've been in direct marketing since 1989. Secondly, I've been helping small to not-so-small businesses and organizations compete and win against rivals with huge marketing dollars. Thirdly, I have a bachelor's degree in sociology from Gujarat State University in India, and an MBA in marketing from Bentley University in Waltham, MA, USA. The reason the last point is important is because sociology is all about the study of relationships and institutions, and marketing is the activities we take to sell our products or services. They go together like peanut butter and jelly.

I published my first book, Business Kamasutra, From Persuasion to Pleasure, The Art of Data and Business Relations in 2015. Since 2002 I've been helping entrepreneurs and business owners build and automate their marketing campaigns by leveraging technology. I have a long and fruitful track record (19 years and counting) of supporting business owners in my community. My clients range from well-known, high-profile direct marketers to local dentists and chiropractors among many other professionals. We have mailed over a billion pieces of direct mail, produced over 10,000 marketing campaigns, built over 1000 websites and landing pages, and generated over 1,000,000 Personalised URL's (PURLS). It has been my privilege to have helped them. This is where my background in sociology comes into play. I love people, I love making friends, and I love helping people with their businesses. The longer I've been in business the more I realize three truths:

1. Many books are buried in detail that overwhelm and confuse business owners and entrepreneurs

2. Although business owners start out with the best of intentions to read everything they can get their hands on about automated marketing processes, most books end up collecting dust on their bookshelves

3. Entrepreneurs and business owners need brief, straightforward, information that gives them the basics in about an hour. They just don't have the bandwidth for anything else that's more involved or time consuming.

I'm always looking for ways to help people learn about systems that produce positive ROI (Return on Investment) for their integrated marketing campaigns. The result of this ongoing endeavor is my book, which focuses on automated lead capture, lead nurture, and relationship development. These things are important for your business because they convert your leads into lifelong customer relationships.

My book is geared towards 95% of business owners who want to solve the question I described earlier in "Who should read this book?"

My book is focused on three truths:

1. It is designed as an overview of the complex and multi-faceted process of creating effective sales/marketing funnels with cutting edge technology, direct mail and shock and awe packages. It is intended to be more like a Marketing Funnels 101 rather than the entire encyclopedia.

2. Reading this book cover to cover will give you a sense of achievement that you now have a grasp of the architecture involved in developing your automated sales/marketing funnel.

3. It helps everyday business owners and entrepreneurs

to understand the processes and systems needed
to develop their own automated sales funnels.

If you've ever wondered how to develop your lead capture, lead nurture, and relationship development through automated processes, but felt it was too complicated or time consuming, this book is your recipe for success. Our excellence is powered by our experience.

Please know I will not be spending any time trying to persuade you that automated sales funnels are the way to go in marketing. I assume, if you are reading this book, you've already convinced yourself and are looking for a breakdown of how the systems can work within your business.

So, grab a coffee, find a comfortable chair, put on your reading glasses, and let me walk you through the journey. If you have any questions or comments, please reach out to me at **www.elaunchers.com/start.**

In gratitude

Parthiv Shah

P.S.: When you've finished reading this book would you please leave a truthful Amazon book review? Reviews are a great way to help others solve the same problem, and I respond to all reviews, and appreciate your feedback.

REMEMBER
TO GET THIS!

For Dentists Only

PART 2

Blueprint for Brent's Automated Sales & Marketing System

CHAPTER 1
You Are NOT
an Elephant

As a professional entrepreneur, you've probably been working very hard for a very long time. It started with your education. Years of schooling. Then you got out into the workplace and realized running a business wasn't something they had taught you in school—and your education started all over again. But you persevered and established a reputation for doing quality work and offering outstanding customer service. Those things you know how to do, and you do them well.

But like all entrepreneurs, bringing in new customers and getting existing customers to return is an ongoing concern. Marketing today focuses on building a relationship through a personalised sales journey that develops the 'know, like and trust factor' for your business. Gone are the days of setting up a storefront and instantly having a customer base that stays with you until you retire. "Nearly 21.55% of the World's population buy online. In 2021, the number is expected to rise to over 2.14 billion." That's where marketing skill and knowledge comes in. It's not enough to have a physical business because you'd be missing out on a large percentage of customers who shop online for products or services.

Now more than ever you need digital marketing skills to determine; WHO buys from you, WHY they buy from you, WHAT they buy from you, and HOW to approach them.

Of course, there are tools that address all of these issues, but they come at a cost. As an online entrepreneur you need to be a master marketer of your website and have the skills (and time) to interpret the analytics that track website traffic, such as reports, page performance, keywords, and competitors. Let's not forget the expert SEO content you are expected to create for your personalised blog posts, and the advanced knowledge of the ever-changing keyword research in your blogs, and blog headings. But that's not all. Email marketing, online products, online sales funnels, landing pages, and social media platforms are a critical part of your branded marketing strategy. You also need to accommodate customers who respond better to direct sales letters and postcards. WHEW!

You need to have the memory of an elephant to store all that information!

Skills aside, how can one person possibly master, let alone remember how, where, and when all the moving parts should be turning to attract, covert, and close leads?

Thankfully, you don't have to because a **Business Relationship system for your ENTerprise** (BRENT) can do the heavy lifting for you. BRENT's structured system includes marketing and sales platforms to help attract visitors, convert leads, and close customers. BRENT can combine a variety of functions which allow marketing and sales activities to be managed all in one place.

Like any system, there is an order and structure and that's what we'll discuss next.

CHAPTER 2

BRENT's Head, Heart, Legs & Trunk

Let's start with the basics. Entrepreneurs know that the best businesses solve a problem. To make things crystal clear, I'll describe what BRENT's head, heart, legs, and trunk tell you about the areas a successful business system follows when applied correctly to problem-solving.

BRENT's Head; Problems are everywhere! Look around your house and yard to see that just about every item in your household solves a problem. We have drinkable water flowing through our pipes so we don't have to dig a well or take hours out of our day to collect water from a stream. Rather than spending vast amounts of time walking to destinations—we have cars that keep us warm and toasty in winter or cool us down in the summer. They luxuriously transport us from one place to the next location. We have clothes for every temperature and location that keep us warm or cool and stylish, as well as protect us from the elements.

As an entrepreneur, BRENT's head represents a working product you have created to solve a specific problem. There are two ways to approach a problem. One approach is to create something novel. For instance, you need to dig a hole to plant a tree, so you develop the idea to speed up the process by inventing a shovel. After using the shovel, you realize it takes quite a bit of time to dig a hole; to speed it up, you create an electric shovel. That second approach is an enhancement — the more familiar the problem, the larger your opportunity.

BRENT's Heart — The heart is where the magic happens. It would help if you were genuinely passionate about solving your customer's problem, bringing it to the world, and be excited about what it can accomplish. Your passion will drive you forward and give you the essential motivation to overcome obstacles that will always present themselves in business. BRENT's heart is where your dream lives and is nourished while you walk, trip and fall, and then get back up on the steppingstones to your path of success.

BRENT's Trunk — Look around you. What problems do you see in your day-to-day life? How would you fix them? Can you brainstorm a novel way of solving the problem? Or can you create a way to resolve the issue with a current solution that takes a few tweaks? Practice looking at problems and seeing them as opportunities in your life. The more you practice this mindset, the more likely you will find a unique solution, and you'll be a successful entrepreneur. BRENT's trunk represents your unique perspective or advantage for sniffing out a new or enhanced solution.

BRENT's Legs — Regardless of your attitude, your business will never get off the ground without forward movement. Several methods can realize forward movement:

Goal setting

- It is a useful tool to measure progress and keep track of your achievements. A business plan is a map that shows you where you are and where you are going. Goals keep you pushing beyond your comfort zone into new areas.

Ongoing learning

- Keeps your mind open and your skills current. Even if you don't have a love of formal classroom training, online training, mentoring, joint venturing, and reading, keep your mind active and engaged.

- Delegating is the difference between effectively breaking through boundaries or having a breakdown from burnout. Delegating increases your productivity and keeps you focused. Instead of trying to do everything yourself, bring on others or automate the tasks you don't have the time, knowledge, or skill to do yourself.

- Keeping on top of new technology is a must in business; all business owners can benefit from understanding the role technology plays in impacting their business. Technology used well saves time, money, and resources.

- As a business owner, you understand the importance of marketing to promote your goods and services in any economy. Creating effective marketing strategies that explore and test products and services will show you what is and isn't working and keep you afloat in the worst and best conditions.

An example of how BRENT engages his head, heart, trunk, and legs at all times for a fully functional and successful business system is a multi seven figure clinical practice with a great reputation in the market for clinical excellence. Patients travel from long distances and check in to a local hotel just to see the fine doctors at this establishment. A well appointed Place Estate gives patients an amazing clinical and creature comfort experience. The clinician is a highly educated individual with significant investment in continuing education. He is an avid reader, astute student and a prolific writer.

There is only one problem: Their Pixel Estate infrastructure ambiance does not match their Place Estate. We did a survey of what the goal of the Pixel Estate (website) was as well as who the ideal patient is.

Using this information we built a much more functional site using HubSpot, allowing for automation, direct downloads of a guide to choose a pain management doctor and direct booking of appointments.

The difference in the website home pages are shown below.

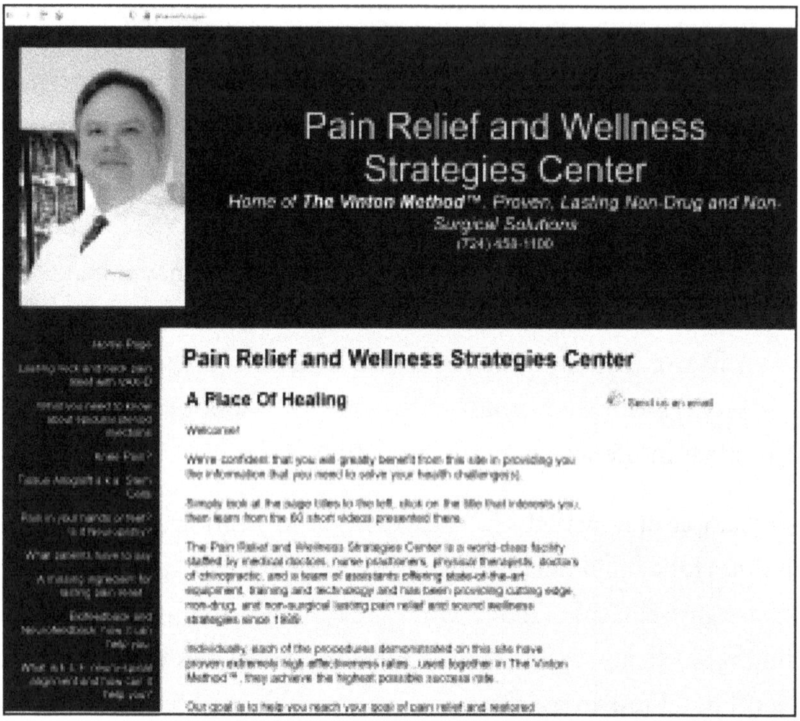

THE VINTON

If you've been struggling for too long to find a long term solution for your pain then it's time to learn about the Vinton Method for pain relief...

Finally A Proven Path To Relief From Crippling Knee, Back, Neck And Joint Pain, Without Drugs Or Surgery

Why Most Treatments Fail   Get Relief Faster

NO More Knee Pain

❝❝

"The pain is mostly gone in my feet. I can sleep at night. I can walk. It used to be I hated to get out of bed in the morning because I knew it was going to hurt my feet and that doesn't bother me at all now. My hands, my fingers aren't numb like they used to be."

Susan

CHAPTER 3
BRENT's
Operating System

The most critical information in your business is knowing your buyer. Who are they? What do they buy? Why do they buy? What must they see, read, hear, and feel before, during, and after they buy? Critical information you need to know about your buyer determines how you will create a compelling and profitable user experience.

> "Dangling the carrot only works if the
> person WANTS a carrot."
> — John Jantsch, *Duct Tape Marketing*

BRENT uses a proprietary "four crystal method" to determine your list research which falls into four areas:

- Customer persona, a fictional character you create that represents your customer type, e.g., married couples, aged 35-45, conservative, two children, and university-educated in professional occupations.

- Market segmentation—categorize your list into segments based on demographics, geography, behavior, personality traits, values, interests, attitudes, and lifestyles.

- Analytics/data science—the methods used to record, store, and analyze usage and provide insightful data.

- Database marketing principles–such as customer lifetime value (CLV), recency, frequency, and monetary analysis (RFM), customer communications, websites, emails, loyalty programs, predictive models, test and controls, among many other predictors.

Crystal 1: Data Sphere

Getting to know your customers involves collecting points of information/data about their needs, wants, and desires. Those data points form data strings, creating the datasheet, which provides a complete buyer persona. Your data sphere should allow you to look at your customer and customer experience from every point simultaneously, which gives you a spherical view of your database.

Crystal 2: Data Pyramid

Not all customer relationships are created equally. Some are more valuable than others. BRENT has developed a proprietary formula based on a customer evaluation money pyramid. The pyramid has two sections. The bottom section is 80% of your customers, who are broke or struggling. The top of the pyramid represents the more well-off 20%.

The 20% beaks into three additional sections; 15% of your customers who earn a good living, 4% who are prosperous, and 1% at the tip of the pyramid who are rich. Once you know where your customer lands on the pyramid spectrum, you can determine how much energy you want to put into that relationship. This method concentrates your efforts on the customers who are most valuable to you and eliminates everyone else.

Crystal 3: Data Prism

Now that you know who should be on which level of your money pyramid, you can create the processes that place your customers on specific pyramid spectrums. Just as a prism takes white light and separates it into a prism/rainbow of colors, a data prism takes universal data and slices it into segments. Individual segments give you knowledge of who, when, where, and what to focus your marketing energy on for the most profitable results.

Crystal 4: Data Cube

The data cube is your digital real estate on the web. It includes your prospects, clients, and influencers. Because they interact with your technology asynchronously, it is called a "touchless sales environment." Your data cube must consist of sophisticated technology that connects your website, blog, landing pages, and sales funnels to your CRM to automate the sales/marketing process. Touchless technology seamlessly choreographs your user experience from welcoming, dispensing personalized content to nurturing, indoctrinating, and monitoring their consumption. Once the customer data assimilates, they know, like, and trust you and are ready for their first conversation with your sales team or can be placed in your automated nurture program.

BRENT's four crystal method identifies your buyer persona, divides customers into most and least valuable, analyzes and segments their data, and automates/connects touchless technology for a powerful and magnetic customer experience.

Identifying and segmenting your buyer list will ensure your marketing process creates an effective and profitable user experience.

I can help you with that right now–download my Implementation Success Blueprint along with the companion CD by visiting www.eLaunchers.com

Sales Pyramid

People say they

% on each level of the Sales Pyramid

01 — are dedicated to hiring whoever it takes so they can evolve, improve, and change the world

04 — are dedicated to doing whatever it takes to evolve, improve, and change the world

15 — want to change and improve but they need a lot of prompting

80 — to change but don't mean it

CHAPTER 4

Unique Content Management System

You understand that your business' marketing system needs more than just one approach to reach customers. You know that coordinating your website, blog, sales funnels, social media, and content is a complicated, time consuming, ongoing, daily process. You can also understand that it's easier to have everything managed from one location than having all of BRENT's parts function independently.

The first place to start is with a unique content management system (CMS) that displays your website and builds relationships with your customers. BRENT's CMS has ten features that provide 10 benefits to both you and your customers.

- It's speedy
  If customers have to wait for your site to load, they'll go elsewhere. BRENT's CMS loads super-fast on any device from any location.

- It's secure
  Unfortunately, getting hacked is a common occurrence and one you'll want to avoid at all costs.
  BRENT's system has Secure Sockets Layer (SSL), CDN locked in, and a security team monitoring the network 24/7. SSL is

the standard technology for keeping internet connections secure and preventing cybersecurity criminals from modifying your information. CDN is a highly distributed content delivery network that enables fast loading times and reliability.

- It analyzes and tracks
  Unless you know what content or products interest your customers, who they are and where they go and stay online, you won't know how to sell to them. Our site includes analytics and tracking in one place

- It has on-page SEO
  Finding the right SEO tools online is a hassle and adds one more step to the complexity of writing copy for an article, a website, a landing page, etc. With our CMS, SEO is included as you write your page.

- It has Smart content
  Smart content is designed to change with your viewers' interests or past behavior for a more personalized customer experience. With our CRM, you can personalize your content based on the demographic, location, device, and language of your anonymous and known visitor characteristics. Smart content converts visitors into customers.

- It has tools to build your online marketing network.
  BRENT's tools help you create your webpages, calls to action (CTAs), pop-up forms, forms, reports, and conversations. BRENT's CRM also publishes your social media posts, targets campaigns, and tells you who needs follow-up.

- It has templates
  Do you want to redesign your website? No problem, BRENT's CRM has content staging. Do you want to develop a new

content strategy? We've got a step-by-step template for that too. Would you like to customize your template? We can walk you through that easily.

- It has contact forms that provide customer insight.
  Would you like to see your customer's activity before they submitted a contact request? BRENT's CRM gives you information on the pages they viewed, how and when they arrived on your website, and how many times they visited your site.

- It has a chatbot
  For customers who want an instant answer, you can add a live chat to answer FAQs.

With BRENT, everything is in one place. You don't need any plug-ins or additional staff to juggle all the moving parts. BRENT's CRM gives you every tool you can imagine, and some you can't, that work with a website that converts viewers into customers.

CHAPTER 5

Unique Customer Relationship Management System

When you started your business, a simple spreadsheet was enough to keep track of your customer information. Then you brought more staff on board. Your receptionist might have had an excellent memory and liked to store some data in her head, other information in her email files, and keep a few paper files. Your sales representative may have kept a spreadsheet. Maybe your accountant kept a stack of invoices in a file folder.

Then your business grew, and some of your original staff left your business, taking customer data with them. Adding insult to injury, the new team took longer to get up to speed because they had to mine for customer information.

As your business grew, your staff had to spend more and more time sifting through emails, files or calling former team members to find customer information. That led to customer service falling between the cracks and getting missed or double-booked. Customer service started to look like a gong show.

Your customers were annoyed because they had to start all over again with new team members. They told you they wanted to have a relationship with your company, not a confusing assortment of shifting people and departments.

That's the importance of storing your customer information in one place where it's accessible to your entire team. A customer relationship management system is a system that (predictably) manages relationships with your customers. These are the challenges our unique CRM system is designed to solve for your business. BRENT's unique CRM;

1. Maintains a central database of your customers and customer leads

2. Enables everyone on your team to have access to the same comprehensive customer information

3. Provides a structured process your sales team can easily follow and tracks their productivity

4. Integrates with the CMS

For your business to provide consistent customer service, your salespeople need to follow a dependable process aligned with your branding. Because of the complexity of current marketing funnels, you should have a reliable method for your salespeople to track where the lead originated. Customers don't appreciate having to repeat the same information every time they talk to someone new from your business. With our CRM, your people can map the source (Facebook, Instagram, blog post), find the question or information the lead provided, and reply to the lead with information or products aligned with their wants and needs. BRENT's CRM connects the dots in a central location.

BRENT's unique CRM system documents every lead and interaction through your website, email, social media, phone calls, and any other channels you use. Our CRM is the brains of BRENT's digital anatomy. It organizes customer information, sales opportunities, and company data.

The more your business scales up, the more critical it is to manage quality customer service and eliminate time and energy drains that frustrate staff and customers. BRENT's unique CRM removes the complexity and streamlines the process for a reliable customer service experience. Staff and customers will appreciate the support and attention to detail. You'll enjoy having BRENT take care of the planning, organizing, and business processes.

If you'd like to discuss how to apply BRENT's unique relationship management system to your business, schedule a strategy session with me by visiting www.elaunchers.com/start

CHAPTER 6
Unique Direct Response Outreach System

Would you be surprised if I told you direct mail gives you a higher return on your investment (ROI) than digital ads? You might be thinking—are you kidding?! That's as outdated and old school as playing music on a cassette player or using an overhead projector for a business presentation!

According to The Data & Marketing Association, in 2016, direct mail had a customer response rate of 43%. ANA.net noted the rapid response rate for mail sent to houses at 5.3% and direct mail sent to prospects at 2.9%. Click through rates for emails average only 2-3%.

Direct mail works. Here's how.

Integrating direct mail and digital marketing is easy and fun

BRENT integrates our unique direct mail system with multiple channels to give you a unique marketing strategy. As savvy marketers, we understand marketing campaigns should span Facebook, Instagram, TikTok, Pinterest, search engine optimized content, and any other channels that your prospects will use and that will increase your traffic and conversion.

An example of this type of integration is to send out a letter or postcard with a QR code that customers can scan with their phone that directs them to your product or service. Or better yet, send them a coupon or gift card, ask them to tweet, take a picture, and post it on your company's Facebook page showing when/how they used it. Integrating direct mail with digital marketing ensures customers are not only using your product but also promoting it to the world.

The added benefit of a coupon or gift card is that it is a physical object that takes up space. My family puts restaurant coupons on the fridge. When we feel like ordering out, guess which restaurant we choose? Think of how many times you used a service or purchased a product because you received a coupon.

ADT used an unconventional direct mail approach. They slid a cardboard letter under house doors that converted into a pop-up box with the message "Breaking into your apartment is easier than you think." Novelty is the single most effective way to capture attention and trigger memory.

A few years ago, I received samples of Voltaren tubes in the mail. I had no idea a topical anti-inflammatory existed. I tried it, liked it, and still use it today.

Direct mail can be seen, touched, smelled, tasted, and heard; it appeals to all the senses from every demographic.

It's easy to target and track your audience

With the US postal service's (USPS.com) Every Door Direct Mail tool, you have access to demographics by area, including average household size, age range, household income, number of residents, and businesses. All this information is available to you by simply hovering your mouse over a route. The bonus is you're reaching every person, of every age, in that household. If you were only using social media, you would have to choose specific social media to target specific demographics. Tracking is easy too and can be easily accomplished by including a unique phone number or landing page for each direct mail campaign and lead followed in your CRM.

Mail is unusual and personal

I have a love/hate relationship with mail. Before the internet, when my wife and I were dating, we relied on phone calls and letters. I still get excited seeing a handwritten note in my mailbox. That's the love portion of mail. I also cringe when I see parking and speeding tickets in the mail, but I still open them. If you're like me, you don't want to miss any bills, which is another reason to open every letter. Like you, I don't receive much mail, and when I do, I always open it, especially if it's handwritten. In contrast, I get hundreds of emails a day and am much less likely to open and read each one.

Because very few marketers send out direct mail, your letter or postcard stands a much better chance of being opened and read.

You might be wondering, what about the customers who don't use your coupon right away? Aren't I just throwing my marketing money away? No, you're not, because when your potential customers receive your direct mail reminders regularly, there may come a day when they need your product or service, or someone asks them to recommend a company with your product or service. They will remember you from your direct mail. If you hadn't sent them anything, they wouldn't know of your existence. Your direct mail sets you apart from your competitors and increases your likelihood of being top of mind.

We choose to integrate direct mail into our customer's unique marketing campaigns because it gives our customers the competitive edge by doing something everyone else isn't doing. Direct mail is a novel, memorable, sensory, fun experience, and above all, it creates a personal touch in an otherwise anonymous world.

I include a case study of HH Hunt Homes below, where we used direct mail marketing. The 4000 pieces of mail resulted in 23 calls, and we sold the house in 9 days!

eLauncher Results

HH Hunt Homes - Website

SUCCESS: MEASURED!

Number of weeks in development: Four

Number of weeks in implementation: Two

Monthly Maintenance Hours Saved: Over 100

ROI: Six months of savings paid for the application

CONVERTING A WEB SITE INTO A CENTER FOR BUSINESS DEVELOPMENT

Sure, the client had a website when we arrived, but the site was born about five years ago in a simple HTML format and over the course of five years the site evolved into about 2700 HTML pages. The team of people working on the website was excellent and there were no broken links and the user experience was never compromised, but the cost of keeping the site updated everyday was just too high. Team eLauncher.com built a custom CMS (Content Management System) and entered all the data from 2683 pages into a set of tables. All documents and images were integrated into a custom DMS (Document Management System). A custom back end allowed client staff to update the site on the fly.

CHAPTER 7

Systems are the Secret to Growth and Freedom

by Clate Mask
Keap CEO & Co-Founder

I would love to tell you that Keap was a phenomenal success from the day we started but like most businesses, the first few years were a struggle. I remember the austere beginnings because it was 18 months after we started our business, in the time leading up to Christmas, that my wife Charisse asked if we were going to have enough money to buy Christmas presents for our four kids. As with most business startups, the first couple of years are the toughest, where you're struggling to grow a customer base and survive on cash flow. My heart sank when I realized that I had to her that "No, we aren't going to have money for Christmas gifts." That sinking feeling got even worse when suggested she do what we used to do in college when we needed to make a little extra money—to throw a bracelet party and get paid to buy the supplies and create the bracelets. And that would give us a few $100 that would allow us to get Christmas gifts.

Guilt is a powerful motivator and at that moment, as I vowed never to disappoint my wife like that again, I realized that the solution had been in front of me for the past 4 months. Our business—Infusionsoft—originally targeted mortgage brokers to help them with their marketing. And, as a way to help them land more clients, one of the things that we had developed at Infusionsoft was the ability to send automated follow-up emails. The feedback we received back from our clients about the effectiveness of the automated email follow-up had all been extremely positive with several claiming it had "revolutionized" their businesses. Curiously, it had never dawned on us to use our own automation to grow our business…

We had been marketing Infusionsoft and had compiled a list of about 1500 contacts so on the evening of my wife's bracelet party, I went upstairs to our loft, and created a campaign that would use our automated follow-up to email the 1500 people on our list. I managed to get the campaign completed but when I was done I realized that I still needed to write the emails. At first, I was deflated by this but then I realized I didn't need to write all the emails that night, I only needed to write the first email because the second email wasn't going to be sent out until a week later. Not only would I have that amount of time to get the next email written and published so that it would go out on time, but I could also send the first email to a portion of the list each day and I could monitor the results and make changes as I received feedback.

The first email went out to our list and I went to work on the second email. A few days after the second email went out I was called by a prospect that had received the emails. He mentioned he had been intrigued with Infusionsoft's follow-up automation and we chatted briefly and I answered his questions. Without warning (and quite surprising to me) he said "Ok. Let's do this." I was stunned. I knew that automation could be a significant asset to a business but I had not realized until that moment, the true power of automation — and, in particular, automated follow-up. To be completely transparent, the contact's statement of "Ok. Let's do this." Caught me completely off guard. So much so that I was fumbling around figuring out what information I needed to process his order.

A few days later it happened to me again. A call seemingly out of the blue, answer a few questions, get an order.

At this point, I went to my partners and with a degree of giddiness announced that we just landed our second order, thanks to the automated follow-up system that we had built into Infusionsoft several months before. My partners, both software engineers, didn't understand the implication or the impact of what I had just told them. Three days later, when it happened again, I recognized it what it for what it was — the Holy Grail that could, if deployed properly, take ANY small business to the Promised Land.

The first principle is "Follow-up works."

As we started to automate our follow-up, Infusionsoft began to grow. We added more automation and recognized that the systems we were building were universal so we moved away from being a specific solution provider for the mortgage industry. Instead, we developed Infusionsoft so that it could be used across multiple industries and niches. As we grew, we aggregated data from our clients and started seeing the patterns and similarities between businesses that were green and growing, and the difference of those that were not.

All of this data allowed us to create a framework called Lifecycle Marketing. The framework is broken down into 3 phases, and each phase is broken down into 3 stages.

The Three Phases Are:

1. Collecting Leads

2. Converting Leads into Clients and

3. Creating Fans.

Collecting Leads Is The First Phase
And Is Comprised Of 3 Stages.

"Study your prospect. Find out what interests
them. Then study your proposition to see how
it can be made to tie in with that interest."

– *Robert Collier*

The first stage is to "target".

A clear understanding of "who" you are marketing your product or service to is critical. At Keap (formerly Infusionsoft), our website's homepage headline is "More sales. Fewer late nights. Grow without the chaos." Our target market is small business owners that are likely struggling with working too many hours, have a feeling of being overwhelmed, and are looking to grow. The headline allows them to self-identify and say "Hey! These Keap people understand me and what I'm going through". When you have clarity of your ideal target market, it allows the prospects to identify you as a business that can help and it provides the insight you need to create the second stage—a method to "attract" that prospect to you.

Next, you "attract" your ideal prospect.

Imagine you're at a reception with hundreds of people. While telling a friend about your son's struggles with mathematics at school, you're tapped on the shoulder and someone you've never met before says "I'm sorry but I couldn't help but overhear about your son's math problems. My name is Jane Doe and I'm a mathematics tutor. I could help your son with…." And they proceed to launch into all the reasons why you should hire them to tutor your son. Now, most people will be backing away from this person mentally if not physically. No one likes being pursued.

But how do you manufacture "attraction"? Consider an alternative conversation. As you're explaining to your friend about the mathematics problem they say "My daughter had a similar problem with math as well. We hired a tutor, Jane Doe, and she was fabulous. She has a unique approach that took our daughter from failing to a B+ in just 6 weeks. Actually, I saw Jane here this evening. She's wearing a purple sequin gown. You should see if you can find her."

Now, you are "attracted" to Jane through the testimonial because you've been given a reason to seek out her expertise. That attraction can be done in other ways where you can leverage automation.

Now it's time to "capture" the name, email, and other information from your prospect.

Most marketing experts refer to this as "presenting lead magnets" with a lead magnet being something that a prospect would be willing to exchange their name and information for. An example might be an offer of a video "5 Proven Strategies To Stop Your Child From Failing Math " or a workbook that teaches "Mathematics — 1 Lettergrade Improvement In Just 15 Minutes Per Night For 1 Week". As a parent myself, if I had a child struggling with mathematics I would gratefully exchange my name and email address for these tools. All you need to do is offer an online form and promise an immediate download, automate the delivery and transition them into the next phase:

Convert Your Prospect Into A Client

They've said "Yes." To your lead magnet. Now it's time to "engage" them and begin to move them to become a paying client.

Engagement is not a hard sell. It's the opposite. When you engage with a prospect you're taking small bits of your product or service and explaining in detail why they would benefit from buying. A key part of engagement is helping them see the outcome of using your product or service. When we first started using the follow-up automation we had developed, we learned very quickly that the emails that generated the most calls contained messages that allowed the prospect to "see" what their lives would be like in the future after they started using our software in their business. This is because people buy emotionally, then use logic to justify their decision. The pricing and technical aspects of Infusionsoft were always presented AFTER we showed them what their future could be like IF they used our software.

> "Make sure that the prospect can visualize every drop of satisfaction that their achievement will give them."
> *– Eugene Schwartz*

While you're engaging with your prospects, you also need to present "offers."

Imagine you need to get some new hiking boots. There's a new outdoor store that has been sending you emails about hiking, overnight camping, and "zero-impact" trailblazing. In the first email, they tell you about local hiking trails and their tent sale. Great information, but not looking for a tent. The next week you get an email about campfire safety and a special 2-for-1 guided hike on a new trail that's just opened. Again, interesting information but you're a super experienced hiker and not interested in hiring a guide. Then a week later you get an email about choosing the best portable gas stove for camping and a special purchase of Oboz Trail Boots at an amazing discount. They tell you about the custom "O-Fit Insoles" Oboz developed to make their boots super comfortable, the waterproof "B-Dry" construction, and the high-traction soles. As a bonus, a tree is planted for every pair purchased. This is the offer you've waited for and you're off to buy a new pair of boots.

Most businesses err by presenting offers that are virtually unchanged from the preceding offer. Most of the time, this is a huge mistake. Even if you only have one product, you can alter your offer. Let's say you're a divorce lawyer. You might be offering a "complimentary 30-minute" consultation. That's great for someone that doesn't want their spouse to see the initial charge on a credit card statement. But what can you do to prevent subsequent charges from appearing? Do you accept cash? What about PayPal? Maybe you have a discreet entrance where clients can come to see you without being followed to your office? Unless you have to ability to ask your prospect directly, you may never know what's keeping them from moving forward and that's how you can use different offers to get to the next step.

The "Close."

Have you ever gone to a car dealership and wandered around the lot looking at cars when the dealership is closed? Statistically, the busiest traffic day for car dealerships is Sunday when the dealerships are closed. Why do we do that? It's because we despise being "sold". It's the feeling we're being manipulated or coerced to do something we're not ready to do. Conversely, people love to "buy". But when Lifecycle Marketing is done correctly, there is no "hard sell closing", no manipulation, and no anxiety. When I received that first call after we sent out the first automated follow-up emails, I didn't "close" the sale. The reality was that I was unprepared when the prospect announced he was "buying". I had taken the time to "engage" with email and send him information that allowed him to see a better future for himself and "offered" to help him achieve these goals by answering his remaining questions on a phone call. He "closed" the sale himself when he said "Ok. Let's do this."

The "close" was easy because it moved him to a future he wanted and he was able to see that the investment he was making in our software would provide him with returns in both time and money that greatly would exceed the price of the software.

Creating Fans.
You've closed the sale but that's just the beginning of your new relationship. Now it's time to "Deliver".

I can't count all the times I've made a major purchase, excited about the future that I've bought, only to be disappointed afterwards. Appliances that didn't show up when promised, a new car with a scratch on it, landscaping that wasn't completed as promised. The most aggravating part was that all of these annoyances could have been easily avoided if the company making the sale had automated systems in place to prevent clients' disappointment.

Automation is about more than just making the sale. When you use automation to trigger events, create tasks for staff, collect and manage payments, and add notes to your new client's records, you maximize the opportunities to stand head and shoulders above your competition. The delivery of your products and services gets done on time, and as specified. When things start to go wrong (which they inevitably all do), you'll have the automated processes in place to keep your clients informed. Mistakes happen. Letting your client know about it and, more importantly, how you're going to fix it will almost always keep your clients from leaving you for another supplier.

That's because automation gives you the tools you need to "impress".

In my life, I've bought more products and services than I can remember. Most of these transactions were adequately performed. You stop for fuel, fill the car and go into the store to get some bottles of water for the family. You pay and leave. No problems. Everything went as expected. Would you ever bring up that transaction at the next family dinner? Of course not. Why? Because it was "as expected". Nothing stood out as exceptional. Compare that experience to a local physiotherapist that uses automation. You arrive at the physiotherapist's office and instead of staying seated and handing you a cheap clipboard and promotional pen, the informed person at the counter stands, addresses you by name, escorts you to a chair and hands you an iPad with most of the information fields already filled out. When you press the "DONE" button at the bottom of the form, the same person comes back, retrieves the iPad and offers you a refreshment while you wait. No sooner does your refreshment arrive than you're being escorted to a treatment room. Total time from arrival — 3 minutes. Sound impossible? With automation it's not only possible, it's possible by small businesses that never dreamed they could actually impress their clients like this. And why do you want to do this? First, this is a business that your clients will WANT to talk about at that next family dinner, as well as to their friends, co-workers, and neighbours. Second, in a world increasingly commoditized and fighting over lower and lower profit margins, you can charge more and your clients will happily pay you for the superior experience. With automation to keep your staff informed, it's all possible.

The best part of impressing your clients is that is even easier to "multiply" them.

There is no question impressing your clients makes it easy to get them to come back again and again. With zero cost to acquire, repeat clients are your most profitable clients. You paid the expensive marketing to bring them in the first time, now you can rely on very affordable email, text messaging and perhaps direct mail offers to get them to come back again and again. These clients are also an excellent source for online reviews and testimonials and because they can't help talking about your business to friends, family and co-workers, they're an excellent source of referrals. Using automation, you can refer them to leave reviews on Google or Facebook, invite them to bring a friend to your next special event, recognize them for being a particular "level" of client, or give them special "offers" for products or services that they can pass along to their acquaintances.

Follow-up works.

Whether you own an established business and are looking to implement more sophisticated systems or you are just starting out and are new to automation, the systems detailed throughout this book will guide you to more sales with fewer late nights and less chaos.

From capturing and converting leads to making sure you get paid on time, Keap's all-in-one Sales & Marketing Automation (SMA) software helps you get more done in less time.

Our partner, eLaunchers has created a special offer just for the readers of this book. When you visit https://www.elaunchers.com/justbuykeap you'll not only have the opportunity to acquire Keap at a special price and with additional users and contacts, you'll also receive:

- FREE 5 Funnels That Have Generated Over $5,000,000 In Revenue To Date & Counting — by eLaunchers.com
- FREE Marketing Automation Campaign — Business Kamasutra by eLaunchers.com (Over 500 installations worldwide)
- FREE Swipe Copy for Campaign, Funnels and Lead Magnets from eLaunchers.com
- FREE Migration from wherever you are to Keap by Keap Migration team.

Go to https://www.justbuykeap.com
and claim your free gifts today.

Clate Mask is the Co-Founder and CEO of Keap CRM Software and lives with his wife Charisse in Chandler AZ.

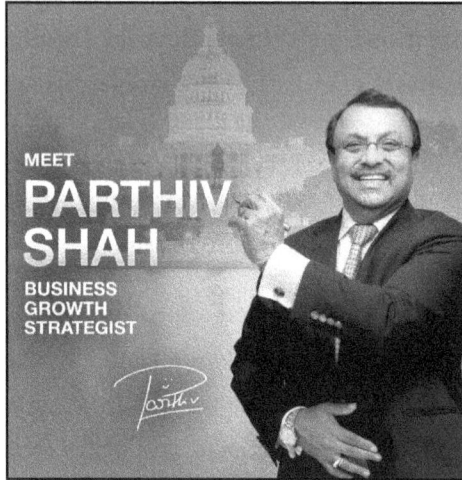

**Book time with Parthiv at
www.meetparthiv.com
and claim your gifts.**

CHAPTER 8
Unique Follow-Up System

Wouldn't it be great if you could make a sale after just one well-done sales presentation?

Typically, your salesperson puts all their energy into doing a great job of the initial sales presentation and then follows up with one phone call or email. That's it. The prospect doesn't buy, and your salesperson believes they are not interested in your product or service and gives up on them. That's how most businesses lose money.

According to a study by Brevet, a sales consulting firm, 80% of sales require five follow-up calls after the meeting. 44% of sales reps give up after one follow-up. 92% of sales pros give up after the 4th call, but 80% of prospects say no four times before saying yes. If your takeaway from these stats is that most customers need well timed and frequent encouragement to say yes by the 5th prompting—you're right.

No one likes being pestered by an aggressive salesperson. Because salespeople don't want to foster that reputation, they assume the prospect isn't interested and back away before they should. But what if their assumption is wrong? What if the prospect has a busy life and receives 300 emails a day and doesn't have the time to read your emails? That's where it becomes essential to have a unique sales follow up system that captures your prospects attention, piques their interest, and encourages them along the path of using your product or service to solve their problem.

BRENT's unique follow-up system uses six methods.

1. Variety

   Effective sales use a system that includes various methods such as phone calls, emails, LinkedIn, or other social media platforms. It's important to remember that different people prefer different follow-up methods. The over 50 demographics may select phone calls or emails; 20-year-olds prefer text or social media. Communicate with them in the way they like.

2. Timing

   Buying decisions take time, and you don't want to annoy your prospect with too many follow-ups delivered too soon. The higher the price tag, and the more people involved in the buying decision, the longer you should allow for your lead time. How often should you follow up? That depends on your prospect. Do they need to connect to a sales manager at Friday's meeting for a final decision? If so, it's best to put the sales meeting date in your calendar to remind you when to follow up.

3. Creates Value

   We hear this message all the time; here it is again. When people know, like, and trust you, they'll buy from you. Use your follow-ups as an opportunity to get to know your prospects so that you can provide value. Have you kept notes on your conversations? Have they told you about their daughter's violin recital? If you ask how it went, they will feel appreciated and valued because you've made an effort to remember. Do you know their business pain points? Can you speak to those issues by providing a solution in a follow-up email with a link to a blog article? Do you have any upcoming sales or special offers? Letting them know is a great way to get them interested and motivated to act.

4. SMART

Specific, measurable, actionable, realistic, and timed follow up is the best way to ensure your unique sales system is following the right steps in the process. Identifying the next steps by setting dates, days, and times moves you towards your goal and your prospect through your sales funnel. Which is more effective; "I'll call you Friday at 9:30 a.m. for a quick 7-minute call" or "I'll get in touch with you in a week."? You guessed it. A specific time and date are always more effective.

5. Get their attention
Re: sales call.

Did that get your attention?

Probably not, because it's boring and could come from anyone. Subject lines need to grab your prospect's attention, with very few words and in a conversational tone. Other useful methods for creating catchy subject lines include:

- Urgency–Your offer expires in 3 hours!
- Novelty–Did you ever do this???
- Showing there is valuable content within the email—"saw this blog and thought it could help you."

Using their first name–just doing this can increase email open rates by 40%

6. Don't waste their time.

   If a busy executive receives 300 emails per day, how long do they have to spend reading them? A minute or two? Keep emails under six lines and phone calls from 5-7 minutes, just long enough to grab their attention and move them towards taking action.

   Know when to call it quits. If you've sent your 5-7 emails/follow-ups and your prospect hasn't responded, move them to a long-term nurture sequence. This is when you send them regular, infrequent information so they keep you in mind for down the road.

   There are skills and science to creating an effective follow-up system, and BRENT's unique automated follow up system does most of the heavy lifting for you in several ways;

7. Lead generation

   BRENT's SMART system tracks who is visiting your site and what interests them while creating custom filters to track qualified prospects. It also provides information on who views your documents and how much time they spend on each one. It can personalize content to the prospect's interests, providing a variety of valuable content.

8. Email automation

   With our system, your email sequences (follow-ups) automate, and you can choose your best emails with the highest response rates. BRENT's system tracks open rates and response rates and selects the best times to send emails to prospects and can stop after any number of sequences you choose.

9. Live chat & calling

While your prospect is interacting with your site, you can get their attention and engage them instantly with live chat, which builds instant rapport and closes sales faster. With our unique system, calls can be scheduled, logged into your CRM, and recorded with just one click.

10. Automated workflow

BRENT's system takes the struggle out of your day-to-day tasks by creating and rotating leads and duties, sending meeting links, and creating customizable SMART reports from your metrics.

Would you like to stop missing 80% of your sales and start maximizing your profit? BRENT's unique follow-up system sets up a streamlined, integrated marketing and sales automation process for your business.

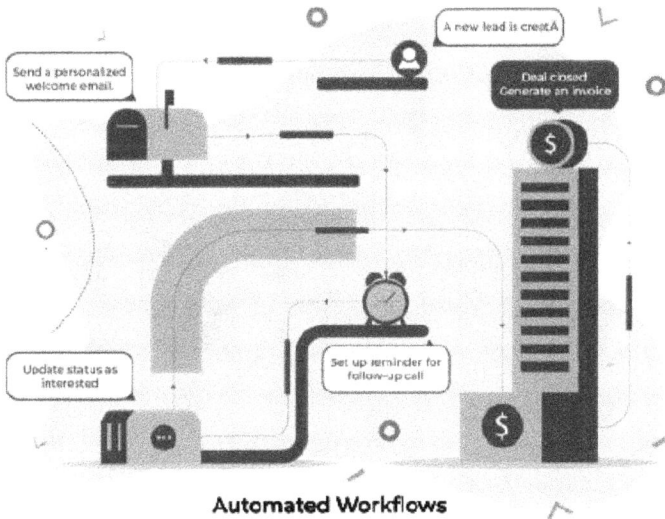

Automated Workflows

CHAPTER 9

Unique Marketing System

E ffective marketing and successful gardening work the same way.

A cactus and a fern are both plants, but if you plant your cactus in the shade and water it as much as you water your fern, it will die. Similarly, if you plant your fern in scorching full sun and water it once a month, you've got yourself a dead fern.

The mistake many marketing programs make is they take every customer and pass them through the same funnels. This system creates friction points as they get bounced around from marketing to sales and, finally, customer service while receiving irrelevant, generic information. Poor service results = low sales.

A typical reaction to poor sales is to inundate existing customers with new products and services, hoping they will buy more and more products. Over working your customers produces the same results as over cultivating your land. The quality becomes degraded, and productivity suffers. Planting more and newer seedlings on infertile soil will not produce a crop of vigorous seedlings.

Recognizing you need new growth to survive, the next reaction is to buy lead lists. If you don't know those prospect's needs, there is little likelihood they will turn into paying customers. If they haven't requested you to contact them, it could hurt your business. Be sure to get targeted lists if you go that route. We can help with those as well.

A successful garden needs fertile soil, healthy seeds, and knowledge of the right amounts of water, sunlight, and nutrients to produce lush, healthy plants. Productive marketing follows a similar process. You need to know and understand your client's needs and wants so that you can nurture their growth with the right kind of information delivered in appropriately timed amounts. Done well, marketing will cultivate a prospect into a flourishing, paying customer.

Once you know your client, you can understand how to attract them with content that is interesting and meaningful to them (inbound marketing), rather than interrupting them with unrelated content (outbound marketing).

Gardening and marketing are all about building ongoing, long-term, personalized relationships. The best marketing systems have your customers' needs and wants at the core, and pair a strategy with customized automation.

Effective marketing collects information about your prospects from multiple channels such as web page activity, social media, and the type of content that interests them. It also uses various channels to build an ongoing relationship. Once your business is at a point where you:

- Know how to create a constant crop of leads
- Understand who should be nurturing your prospects at which phase of their growth
- Recognize your client's needs from their digital fingerprint across

multiple channels

- Have figured out successful lead tactics and are ready to scale up;

Then you're ready for our unique marketing system.

BRENT's unique marketing system allows you to:

1. Create personalized workflows to segmented lists of clients from your CRM

2. Build tailored emails and generate email drip campaigns (scheduled emails that keep you in touch)

3. Automate tons of mundane tasks such as lead rotation and data management–to free up your time

Our unique one-stop inbound marketing software enables;

- easy publishing of search engine optimized, appropriate, appealing blog content

- optimized, personalized landing pages

- tailored emails, content, and subject lines

Lead management

- for sales-ready, focused campaigns

- analytics for social media, SEO, calls-to-action, and advertisements that let you measure and assess your customer progress and your ROI

- Synchronization of datasets for easy access to emails, CTA's, forms, and segmented lists

When marketing operates in a silo, productivity suffers. For marketing to produce a healthy crop of flourishing customers, it requires a unique, integrated, organic system specific to the customer within a multi-channel dynamic ecosystem.

CHAPTER 10

Unique Sales System

Your sales staff carry a heavy load. Every day they prospect to find leads, follow up on leads, score leads, send out emails, log calls, and schedule appointments. They put together sales quotes and proposals, onboard customers, record conversations and notes on prospects, and request approvals—all while staying on top of products, services, and pricing. Most of their tasks don't make them or your business any money. Non-revenue producing activities make the most sense to automate. Automating frees up your sales staff to focus their efforts on doing the things that bring in the most income.

Sales automation is software that automates mundane, repetitive tasks such as prospecting, creating and sending emails, email campaigns, updating contacts, setting up appointments, recording sales calls, and creating reports.

Let's look at a day in the life of "Bob," your sales representative.

Bob starts his day by spending a couple of hours looking for prospects on LinkedIn and Sales Navigator.

He knows his ideal customer profile and fishes through hundreds of profiles to find the most qualified prospects by industry.

He then takes another hour to check his prospect's social media profiles to understand better who they are, what they want, and what method of communication they prefer. Once he has his list, he takes approximately 50 minutes to enter their data into his qualified leads spreadsheet manually.

Bob's next step is to start emailing or calling. He has done this work for years, and he has an excellent telephone message and a standard introduction email. He manages to reach six people on his list of 20; four of them ask him to call/email them back on specific days/times. Bob takes 30 minutes to enter their follow-up dates and times into his online calendar. Then he spends another 40 minutes creating email follow-ups with some of his other prospects that were scheduled into his "to do" list. He documents his calls and emails in his spreadsheet which takes approximately 30 minutes.

The favorite part of his job (besides closing sales) is creating proposals and sales quotes for his hot leads. He has several bids and quotes in his databank, and he cuts and pastes information from several documents and personalizes the selections before emailing them. This task typically takes him an hour.

Bob spends the last part of his day creating sales reports for his manager, who likes to stay in the loop and adds them to his weekly sales meeting. Sales reports average 1 hour.

If we break down Bob's activities:

Prospecting 2 hours

Social media research 1 hour

Data entry 50 minutes

Emailing/phone calls 1 hour

Scheduling appointments 30 minutes

Administrative tasks 30 minutes

Quotes/proposals 1 hour

Reporting 1 hour

Total hours 7 hours 50 minutes

Total hours spent on direct sales for warm/hot leads 2 hours

Total hours spent with administrative tasks 5 hours 50 minutes.

What if Bob could flip his schedule around and spend 5 hours and 50 minutes on the activities that make him and the business the most money and only 2 hours or less on the other activities? Would that increase your profits? You bet it would!

Our unique sales system has a custom filter through LinkedIn or Sales Navigator where Bob can enter his prospect criteria. It automatically sends him the prequalified list daily, weekly, or monthly. It also pulls data from his prospect's social media profiles, CRM records, surveys, webinar participants, Facebook Lead Ads responders, and new email subscribers. Now he has a full overview of his prospect's responsibilities, company size, industry, vendors, interests, and needs. Because it automatically inputs and organizes the data in his CRM, he doesn't have to keep hundreds of spreadsheets or spend hours entering data.

Emails are a breeze with BRENT's unique sales system which can create email templates and personalize them with the prospect's name, company, and job title. It can queue up Bob's email campaign and even add tailored details to make them sound as if Bob wrote them himself.

For a follow-up, rather than wasting time emailing back and forth to find a mutually convenient time, Bob can send a calendar link to his prospect, and they schedule a time that suits them. Bob never has to worry about forgetting a call or appointment since our sales system schedules reminders. Once on a call, Bob's sales calls can be recorded, transcribed, and logged in his CRM.

Finally, with our sales system, cutting and pasting is a thing of the past. When Bob creates a quote, all the essential details such as customer information, product information, and service or product details automatically transfer to the CRM.

Bob's manager can also save time and energy with BRENT's sales system. Our CRM can create automated reports he can send to his team. Our system scores and rotates leads that he can choose to assign by territory, company size, or any other criteria he chooses.

With BRENT's unique sales system on your side, your sales staff can focus on the work that makes the most profit and "outsource" the time consuming, unprofitable tasks to our automation.

CHAPTER 11

Unique Finance System

Generating new, qualified leads is the lifeblood of any business. Your ability to analyze each lead's cost, product, or sales funnel with your ROI is a critical factor in your success as a business owner.

Consider these facts:

- Using account-based marketing—a method that targets key people within relevant industries to your ideal target base – *is recognized by 92% of companies as a B2B must-have* (Source: DemandBase).

- *47% of B2B buyers read 3-5 blog posts or pieces of content before engaging with a salesperson* (Source: DemandGen Report).

- Reading isn't the sole method of capturing your customer's interest; viewers retain 95% of a message when watching it in a video, compared to 10% when reading it in a text (Source: Insivia).

- Cold calling, flyers, and events are outbound marketing tactics that most companies use to attract clients. Although outbound marketing is a valuable component of a marketing strategy, it is more time consuming to personalize. It takes much longer for customers to get to know you and your brand.

- Email remains a crucial channel in B2B marketing.

- Bringing in new customers is critical, and attracting leads is crucial to business growth.

- The cost for buying leads varies significantly between industries. Prices can be as low as $16/lead for non-profits and as high as over $600/lead for traditional advertising.

- Your existing customers are your highest growth potential.

From these facts, we know:

- You should spend your time targeting your ideal customer because you and your sales team don't want to lose time and money on irrelevant leads.

- Customers like to read several relevant blog posts before engaging with your business, and they want personalized content.

- If you have important information you want your customers to retain, a video is the best delivery method.

- Adults only want to read the information that is relevant and practical to them. They don't have the time to sift through unrelated information.

- Most budgets don't allow for $600 per lead, and you have to attract quality leads through the most cost-effective means available.

- You should concentrate effort on your existing customers to nurture them through your sales funnel.

What's your ROI?

What you pay for leads, of course, is relative to your ROI from the actual lead. If you price your service or product at $12,000 and you can close on 40% of your leads, $600 per lead isn't an issue. If your product or service is $500, and you close at 40% of your leads, $600 is an insane price.

It makes sense that the higher your ROI, the higher the lead's price. Similarly, the smaller your ROI, the less you can budget for leads.

All Leads Are Not Created Equal

Marketing leads are typically segmented into two categories: Marketing Qualified Leads (MQL's) and Sales Qualified Leads (SQL's). MQL's capture the interest of potential customers. SQL's are when a potential customer shows interest. To turn the SQL into a customer, you need to have the right product, the right price, and the customer is willing to pay the money to buy your product/service.

Once you have that information, your cost for producing leads depends on many factors, including which channel you advertise, the quality of your content, who you are targeting, and how you are targeting potential clients. Split tests or A/B testing are processes where you try out two versions of the same web page, email, article, or advertisement to see which does better. The cost of conversion is roughly 2%-10%.

The other option is to generate leads yourself with BRENT's unique finance system.

In any business, you have five types of contacts: Visitors, Strangers, Leads, Customers, and Promoters. BRENT's inbound system targets your ideal customers and converts them into your customers and promotes organically by nurturing them through the funnel. Our system crafts buyer personas and creates lead flows and smart SEO content. Inbound marketing also taps into your existing customers and makes profits through an effective sales funnel.

Smart content personalizes their experience, solves their problems, and moves them forward in their journey towards engagement. For example

- When potential customers are still considering your product/service, you can target your content to focus on products or services that provide solutions to their problems, such as case studies or webinars.

- When potential customers have decided, your content can focus on the key differentiators, such as pricing, free trials, and demonstrations.

Lead magnets with evergreen content (information is rarely if ever needed to be updated) are a cost-effective, long-term way to boost your website by attracting new qualified prospects. Content pillars (content focused around a subject or keyword) feed into BRENT's system to establish you as a subject matter expert. BRENT's system can then optimize your content with on-page SEO. It plots your inbound campaign, allocates specific/personalized content to campaigns, segregates your list for targeted campaigns, tracks performance, and generates reports on goals and key performance indicators (KPIs).

When you have essential information that would perform best in a video format, BRENT's system can insert and embed video content with video tutorials, testimonials, Q&A's, news, and updates. BRENT's system allows preview functionality across multiple devices, sends out your social media marketing from one location, and even drives paid ad campaigns. BRENT's service hub unites all messages across all channels for easy access and increased collaboration.

BRENT's unique financial system gives you a competitive advantage to generate and mine leads. While supporting your content creation, it streamlines your marketing campaigns and integrates your essential marketing tools and platforms.

CHAPTER 12
Unique Referral System

Picture your potential customer hunting for a product or service, where are they most likely to look?

Besides the internet, people often turn to their family, friends, and colleagues. If you have provided excellent service, your customers will be happy to refer your product or service to their friends, family, and colleagues.

Referrals are essentially word of mouth marketing that is very powerful and effective. When a potential customer hears how great your business is from a raving fan, it carries more weight and credibility than when you tell them the same thing. Referrals from a trusted source have a high level of confidence. 92% of consumers trust recommendations from friends and family above all other advertising forms (Source: Nielsen Global Media). Additionally, nearly 95% of shoppers read online reviews before making a purchase (Source: Spiegel Research Center). New businesses frequently get their foothold with new clients, with 20-50% of their sales coming from referral business. (Source: McKinsey & Company).

Because referrals build on existing relationships with your most loyal customers, referrals foster even deeper loyalty. Since referral marketing has a lower customer acquisition cost (CAC) than most marketing, you can increase your revenue by building on your existing customer base. From dentists and doctors to clothing and consulting services, referral programs can bring in a steady stream of new customers.

Getting your best customers to remember to spread the word to qualified customers requires a systemized approach. This approach must always encourage and remind customers that providing referrals is not just the right thing to do but the expected thing to do. A referral program can serve as a reminder to guarantee results. Following these steps will set you on the right path:

1. Set sales targets for how many referrals you would like to achieve each month

2. Determine where your referral sources are originating

3. Identify all potential referral sources

4. Specify your ideal client and make it clear to your referrals

5. Choose appropriate channels to host your referral program

6. Select your referral rewards and always say thank you

7. Create messaging, notifications, and resources for your customers

8. Create a follow-up plan for your referrals

Sales Targets

Do you want your referral program to bring in new customers/revenue? If so, how many and how much? Or do you want your referral program to increase customer loyalty? Each requires a specific approach.

Dropbox's referral program offered an extra 500 MB of free storage to the referral and the new customer. The result? A whopping <u>increase</u>

in membership by 60% in 2010. (Source: infinitive). Uber assigns personalized referral codes (Source: Uber) and rewards both the new and existing customer with a free trip when the new account is activated.

Referral Sources

A referral source system that builds into your marketing funnel from the onset enables you or your sales team to have a history of where the referral originated and track and reward the referring customer.

Evernote's referral program rewards existing customers with points that can be redeemed for premium features and gives additional points if referrals upgrade to Evernote Premium. (Source: Evernote).

Potential Referral Sources

Referrals don't just have to come from existing customers. They can come from vendors, former customers, or leads from LinkedIn or other social media. Anyone you have a contact within the present, past, or future could be a potential referral source.

Your Ideal Client

Before your customers go out and do the leg work for finding you referrals, make sure they know who to refer. Have a clear description of your ideal client front and center on your referral program so that they can send you qualified leads or customers.

Verafin, a fraud detection and anti-money laundering software company, included a "Referral Certification" to educate customers on Verafin's ideal referral client in their month-long contest. The results? 117 quality referrals. (Source: influitive).

Choosing Appropriate Channels

To make your referral program perform, you need to choose an appropriate channel to notify your customer and your business when a referral is captured. Facebook, WhatsApp, Facebook Messenger, WeChat, and numerous other social media channels have a referral landing page with pre-populated messages that include the offer, a referral link, and the company's social media ID or tag — to monitor messages. Social media is an excellent channel for impulse behavior. Most people use at least one of the channels to stay in touch with friends, kill time, look for entertaining content or catch up on the news. Because they're there for fun, it's easier for people to act on impulse.

Referral Rewards

The best referral programs do one of two things; offer cash incentives or non-cash incentives.

1. Air BnB's Travel Credit program offers cash incentives by providing an Air BnB coupon towards the next qualifying reservation.

2. Tesla offers non-cash incentives for something money can't buy. Tesla gifts a referral prize with a 'one of a kind", Powerwell 2 battery for the first person to refer 20 people in their region.

Different people respond to additional incentives. It's essential to put some thought into what would motivate your existing and potential customers to send referrals your way.

Create Messaging and Resources

Once you've created your referral program, it's time to generate newsletters, blogs, product updates, and emails for each of your referral contacts that explain your referral program. These resources should link to your landing pages and workflow for your sales funnels. Like all effective sales funnels, personalization and persistence are key.

Follow Up

When your referrals send you a lead or customer, be sure you have an efficient automated sales process in place that allows you to follow up with them immediately and say thank you. If you don't, there's a good chance your competition will. The sooner you get back to your referrals, the better your chance of converting them into your customer. In addition to incentives, do remember to thank your referral source, they'll appreciate it. And if you don't, they'll notice it and probably not send anymore referrals your way.

Have a look at your customer base; chances are you have many happy customers who would be thrilled to refer business to you, especially with attractive incentives. All you need to do is make the first move by creating a referral culture. BRENT comes to the rescue with its integrated, high conversion, autopilot marketing system that utilizes a systemized, digital referral approach. BRENT's referral system reinforces and ingrains a referral culture with your clients.

CHAPTER 13
Technologies to Empower Your Brent

My friend Gil grew up on a dairy farm in the 1960s. His parents bought a farm that came with an ancient three-bedroom house. When they had their first couple of children, it worked fine. However, when they had more kids than bedrooms, his Dad realized he needed a bigger house, so he started adding extensions.

He didn't worry about drafting blueprints, building codes, fire regulations, electrical codes, or any of those other silly things. He kept adding extensions until they stopped having children.

The result was a jumble of a Frankenhouse. Some bedrooms had too much heat; some bedrooms had no heat. There were two bathrooms. The one upstairs had no heating, and a bathtub, the new one on the main floor had the luxury of heat and a shower. There were two kitchens; one had the modern amenities, including running water and heat, the old kitchen had heat but was always cold. There was no basement, so the main floor was freezing.

The house was in a constant state of renovation. When his Dad started digging to add a new extension, he frequently hit the phone line, which cut off the entire neighborhood's telephone connection.

Many organizations "plan" and "organize" their software systems the same way as Gil's Dad built his house. It's not a criticism; it's a reality.

When Gil's parents started a family, they were so busy earning a living and raising seven children that they built additional rooms as quickly and cheaply as possible to accommodate their growing household. When you start a business, you are so busy keeping all the balls in the air that you grab a quick software solution when a problem appears.

Over time, more issues pop up, and so do software fixes. Because they are not designed to be integrated, you cobble them together with various third-party applications. Much like Gil's family home, your software ends up resembling a "Frankensoft" environment.

Although Frankensoft allows you to choose and deploy the best software from multiple companies quickly, it has significant drawbacks. In Gil's family home, the rooms did not integrate with a central heating, electrical, and plumbing system, which meant something was always missing or breaking down, and the house was unsafe.

The same thing happens to your Frankensoft environment. Patching up all the little things that continually break down becomes more expensive in the long run than if you had paid for one or two more significant programs with a couple of vendors. Frankensoft also becomes a nightmare to support because vendors don't necessarily know how to or want to support each other's programs.

Eventually, Gil's parents sold the farm to a carpenter who rebuilt the house according to code. It's now a beautiful, structurally sound, fully functional, safe farmhouse.

Eventually, your Frankensoft system will break down and harm or destroy your business efficiency and growth. Sooner or later, you will have to face a final reckoning and rebuild your TechDeck, starting with a blueprint of what your businesses plan, marketing strategy, marketing plan, and user workflows require.

BRENT takes the legwork and guesswork out of selecting the right software. We've done the research and found the most efficient and cost-effective tools that attract visitors, convert leads, and support inbound marketing. The technologies used to empower your BRENT include:

1. Hubspot
   This is an "all in one" tool for inbound marketing and sales. It attracts visitors and converts prospects into qualified leads who then turn into customers. It integrates numerous functionalities such as email and eCommerce automation, social media, keyword research, and website analytics. It works well with small and mid-sized businesses that already have a sales team and want to attract and maximize sales through a funnel. It saves you time and money by centralizing your marketing, sales, and customer service departments.

2. Keap
   Is an automated CRM, email, and e-commerce sales tool for small businesses. It allows you to manage and optimize your customer relationship lifecycle through marketing/email automation, lead capture, and e-commerce.

3. Click Funnels
   As its name suggests, allows you to build your entire sales funnel, sell and promote your products online. It does this by automating your sales process from beginning to end.

4. Mailbox Power

    This is a print automation engine connected to your CRM
    so you can send out printed post cards, sales letters, greeting
    cards, small edible gifts and non-trivial personalized gifts
    AUTOMATICALLY by simply checking off a button in your
    Keap or HubSpot. (An automation in Mail Box Power is
    triggered by a Zap in Zapier).

5. WordPress

    is a free and publicly accessible (open-source) website building
    and content management software platform. You can add
    plugins to the website to provide additional functions such as
    Yoast, which helps you optimize your SEO content. Another
    example is WPForms, a plugin that enables visitors to input
    their information so you can get in touch with them.

Which one of these is best for your business? Although it sounds
like a cliché, your business is unique, which makes your business
needs unique. Mapping out your business plan, marketing strategy,
and marketing plan while defining your customers and staff will
determine your user flow. These factors will then set the stage for
creating the blueprint for your TechDeck.

With the knowledge you have gained from this book, you can
implement these processes and systems yourself. If you reach out to
my office, I will happily help you map out your campaign blueprint to
implement the workflow yourself or hire a consultant to implement it
for you. I will even provide guidance and advice to help you choose
a consultant. When I'm not making money, I'm making friends; I
need them both.

CHAPTER 14
BRENT Climbs the Pyramid

When a person has a problem, do they immediately think—I'm going to buy something right now to solve it? Impulse buying excluded; a trigger propels them to take action to have it resolved. The trigger is the start of your customer's buyer's journey on the path they travel to find a solution. The customer journey has three phases;

1. the attraction/awareness stage

2. the engagement/consideration stage

3. the final destination or delight/decision stage

In the attraction/awareness stage, you attract strangers who know they have a problem, but they don't know about your service or product. It solves a problem that either;

- they haven't been able to figure out themselves

- are too busy to figure out themselves

- don't want to figure out themselves

In the engagement/consideration stage, strangers have become prospects who know of your product/service, have experienced some aspect of it, and are weighing their options before deciding to purchase.

In the final delight/decision stage, prospects turn into customers who have decided to purchase your product with a strong call to action. If they are delighted with it, they will buy it multiple times.

To understand the journey, you need to understand your customer persona, pain points, obstacles, wants, needs, and budget. You also need to know where they are positioned on the sales pyramid to attract them.

Generally speaking, with any group of customers, there are four levels in a pyramid structure:

1. The 80% who want to change but don't mean it

2. The 15% who say they want to change and improve but they need a lot of prompting

3. The 4% dedicated to doing whatever it takes to evolve, improve, and change the world

4. The top 1% dedicated to hiring whoever it takes so they can evolve, improve, and change the world

The pyramid base is where the 80% live — those who say they want to change but generally don't ever get there. The next level of the pyramid is the 15% who want to change and improve but need a lot of prompting to reach their destination. The 2nd closest station to the top is the 4% who are willing to do whatever it takes to evolve, improve, and change the world. The top 1% of the pyramid have the money to hire whoever it takes so they can develop, improve, and change the world.

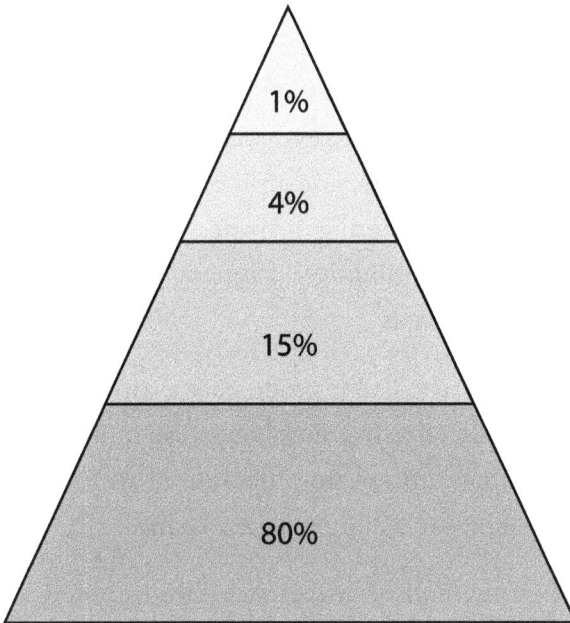

Within the pyramid structure is a marketing strategy. The marketing strategy for each of the three phases in the buyer's journey addresses specific goals. BRENT has a four-phase system for climbing the pyramid.

1. How BRENT tackles the 80%

At the bottom of the pyramid, BRENT's attraction system uses five tools; SEO digital content, tripwires, ascension marketing, qualification marketing, and automated conversion.

BRENT starts the climb with SEO digital content that shows prospects how to solve their problems. Blog posts, eBooks, whitepapers, how-to videos, tools, tip sheets, educational webinars, and social media content are excellent tools to capture attention and move prospects forward in the buyer's journey.

With BRENT's pre-qualification tool, prospects are filtered, prequalified, and sorted into daily, weekly, or monthly lists. It also pulls data from qualified prospect's social media profiles, and CRM records, surveys, webinar participants, Facebook Lead Ads responders, and new email subscribers. BRENT's qualification marketing provides a full overview of your prospect's responsibilities, company size, industry, vendors, interests, and needs.

A low priced, irresistible product, or a tripwire, is another tool that is highly effective, simply because it offers massive value and costs next to nothing. Because of its low risk and high value, people are willing to take a chance.

The best method of attracting your customers and keeping them is by encouraging them along the pyramid either vertically or horizontally. BRENT begins by offering an inexpensive product first where they can get a taste for what you offer. A low-priced product/service doesn't involve a lot of justifying, because it doesn't cost much, so the risk is low. After they have experienced your product, you have built up their know, like, and trust factors and they will be willing to invest in the next higher priced product. Your products can continue to climb in price until finally, they are at the top level. When they reach this level, they will be your long-term client for years to come, if you continue to provide quality products and services. The faster you move people through these levels, the higher your profit.

The Ascension marketing tool allows prospects to advance from a lower priced product to higher priced products. To advance, they must buy the entry level product or the tripwire product first.

Movement along the pyramid can be horizontal as well as vertical.

With horizontal movement, after the first \$19.99 product you can offer a 2nd level of courses/CDs for \$39.00 in five or six different areas that relate to the same topic. This way your client is gaining a breadth and depth of information and will buy multiple times on the same level.

Let's say you want to move your clients vertically. First you advertise an ebook on Facebook for \$19.99. The 2nd product is a hardcover book and a CD for \$39.99. The 3rd product is a course and one coaching session for \$3,900, and the 4th product is a six-month course with individual weekly coaching sessions for \$39,000.

Once people have bought a product or service from you, they are open to buying again and at a higher price as long as you are providing value. They will also buy products you recommend. In their eyes, you have identified yourself as an authority they know, like, and trust.

Throughout the process, BRENT's automated conversion tool systematises the time-consuming repetitive tasks. Qualifying website leads, emailing, social media posting, personalising emails, and converting prospects into profitable customers is in BRENT's wheelhouse.

2. How BRENT tackles the 15%

To attract the 15% level of the pyramid who want change

but need prompting, BRENT employs three hardworking strategies; Sprocket Rocket APP (SR APP), Business Kamasutra, and Integrated Marketing Management (IMM).

Sprocket Rocket App (SR App) uses drag and drop pre-built, customizable website pages, landing pages, and blog page builders that are specifically designed to attract your cold, warm and hot prospects. It integrates with all BRENT's features including CMS, local website development, mobile optimization, website pages, and website themes. It is the flirtation phase of the attraction process for these 15%.

Business Kamasutra is an integral theme of BRENT's attraction and retention system and is designed to nurture and build lifelong relationships with prospects, customers, marketing channels, and affiliates. It follows the same processes people practice when seeking a soulmate and progresses through the attraction phase to engagement and delight.

During the mating process people segment their markets, identify prospects and then plan-prepare-orchestrate, and execute a (hopefully) perfect approach. If all goes well, they seek consent to engage in a dating ritual where both parties share information about each other. At that point when they have established enough trust to seek consent for intimacy, they engage in foreplay, and when ready, engage in the mating ritual. BRENT's Kamasutra business path is designed to follow the self-same path to a long-lasting and mutually fulfilling relationship.

It isn't always easy to attract a suitable partner, and that's where a matchmaker who knows everybody and can connect them comes in handy. Integrated marketing management or IMM is part of BRENT's business strategy to integrate people, processes and technologies seamlessly in lifelong relationships.

3. How BRENT tackles the 4%

Since the 4% dedicated to changing the world are already motivated, and can buy more from you, they are your high value client (HVC). The more products or services they buy from you over their lifetime, the more valuable they are. In short, they have a high lifetime value (LV). Attracting this level of the pyramid requires a more nuanced approach. BRENT's system uses a master sales presentation to tell a compelling story that aligns with your prospect's needs and desires and highlights your product or service's value proposition. Although it ends with a forceful call to action, instead of leading to a sales funnel, it leads them to your unique characteristics that show you as the definitive choice. It does all this through BRENT's automated IMM.

4. How BRENT tackles the 1%

The 1% of the pyramid, and the most coveted, may have already found a solution with your rivals. It's up to you to convince them your product or service is superior. Acquiring these clients is called conquest marketing because you are targeting customers outside of your regular base. BRENT accomplishes this with conquest letters and conquest shock and awe.

BRENT's conquest sales letters capture hearts and minds which create opportunities to hear and experience the power of your product/service. BRENT's conquest strategy captures data on what the competition is doing. BRENT then shows your 1% prospects a solution their competitor does not offer that makes your service/product seem more valuable. BRENT approaches this from where your prospect is positioned in your sales funnel (attraction, engagement, delight).

As an example, a "shock and awe package" is delivered to your prospect before they have bought anything. It is filled with books, CD's, lead magnets, and reports targeted to providing solutions. It establishes you as an expert in your field. It's sent by mail—because who doesn't love getting a package in the mail filled with useful gifts? The shock and awe package strategy is highly effective because it gives prospects something rather than asking for something, and impresses them with your knowledge and expertise.

To delight new customers, include a personalized video via email welcoming clients and showing them how to get the most out of your product/service. As a reminder of why they should continue doing business with you, anniversary gifts sent to clients to celebrate when they became a customer will invoke shock and awe.

BRENT's system develops sales funnels around your industry and audience intent that maps personalized content to each phase of your customer's buyer journey.

BRENT climbs the pyramid with automated and personalized tools and strategies that build awareness and engage and delight customers at every level of the pyramid.

PART 3

Hi, I am **BRENT**
e
launchers
eLaunchers.com

Information Needed
to Put Brent All
Together

CHAPTER 15

RFM and the Customer Value Matrix

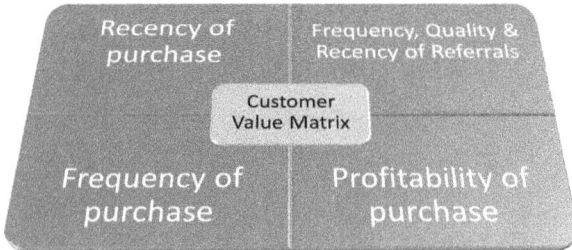

M eet Luis Chocolat, fifth-generation chocolatier, and purveyor of Louis' Haut Chocolat, fine Belgian chocolates. Three years into the business, Louis knows his customers really well and sees common trends.

- There's Sophia — a self-described diehard chocoholic. Sophia views Louis' Haut Chocolat as an essential food group and orders Ben's chocolates every month through his automatic "Chocoholic" monthly program. Sophia is a successful luxury realtor and always includes Ben's chocolates in her "welcome home" gift baskets or "thanks for your business " baskets for her clients. She also loves to send Louis' Haut Chocolat to friends and family for special occasions. Sophia buys regularly and spends at least $5000 every month.

- When Ben got a phone call from the NHL for 5000 personalized packages for their gala awards night, he was over the moon. The NHL told Ben if they received good feedback from the gala, they would place at least one large order per year. The NHL has only bought once, but they spent $250,000.

- Among Ben's customers are family and friends like Natalie and Alan, who like to treat themselves to a small box of truffles every month. Louis knows they enjoy gifting family and friends with Louis Haut Chocolat, and he can always count on them to buy one box of truffles for Christmas and Easter. Natalie and Alan buy recently and often, however since they are on a budget, they don't ever spend more than $40 per transaction

- Lastly, he has a couple of large businesses who threw lavish Christmas parties and spent over $10,000 per order for two years; however, since COVID, he hasn't heard from either of them.

The overview of customer behaviour Luis has noted a marketing term called The RFM Value Matrix, an acronym for Recency, Frequency, and Monetary Value. With this behavioural system, Louis can create, analyze, estimate, and assign a numerical value from lowest to highest for each customer. With this system, he can reasonably predict which customers will buy his chocolates in the future and on who or where he should focus his attention.

The RFM Customer Value Matrix:

According to the RFM Customer Value Matrix;

"A" Customers — are the shoppers who earn the highest score in each of the recency, frequency, and monetary value categories. Sophia would definitely qualify as Louis' "A" customer.

"B" Customers — these are the customers who may have only bought Louis' chocolates once but spent a lot. For Louis, The NHL is his "B" customer.

"C" Customers — are the lowest spending group who regularly transact, such as Natalie and Alain, who is steady, loyal clients on a budget.

"D" Customers — these customers bought frequently and spent a lot, but they haven't bought anything from Louis since the start of COVID.

Louis decides to segment his customer list into three categories with four tiers each;

Recency	Frequency	Monetary
Tier 1	Tier 1	Tier 1
Tier 2	Tier 2	Tier 2
Tier 3	Tier 3	Tier 3
Tier 4	Tier 4	Tier 4

Louis discovers 64 recognizable customer segments.

Communicating Effectively with Each Segment

Louis knows from experience that each of his four types of clients responds to a unique type of communication. He knows all customers don't want to hear about all offers all the time. If he marketed the smaller, less expensive items to Sophia, she would be insulted. Similarly, if he tried to market the Chocoholic program to Natalie and Alain, they would probably drop off thinking they can't afford that type of monthly expense. Likewise, a monthly membership to the NHL does not fit with their needs or buying pattern. So, the next step for Louis is to choose the type of tailored communication he will send to each group, based on their historical behavioural patterns.

This is how Louis decides to communicate with each customer segment;

"A" Customers — Louis gears his communication towards making Sophia and others like her feel valued and appreciated. Since Sophia accounts for a high percentage of Louis' business, he wants to ensure he keeps her happy and exceeds her expectations. He knows he will need to continually analyze Sophia's preferences and her customers' preferences to provide more personalized messaging and custom monthly membership packages.

"B" Customers — Louis wants to treat this segment with kid gloves and nurture them along their path. His messaging will make them feel special and valued and offer them tantalizing incentives to continue doing business with him.

"C" Customers — Louis appreciates his repeat low spending customers and will tailor his communication to let them know he values their business while rewarding them with special offers and incentives to increase their spending.

"D" Customers — Louis' communication will involve reassessing their current needs to discover how to best communicate with them so that they will re-engage with his business.

RFM is an excellent tool to predict customer behaviour based on past customer behaviour; however, ongoing communication is needed to indicate future activities and preferences accurately.

The RFM Customer Value Matrix is an excellent tool to show Louis which customer segment his revenue comes from so that he can focus his efforts on keeping the top revenue generating clients happy. An RFM analysis also indicates "whether a person who buys twice every six months might be better than a person who only bought once in three months. The most recent, the most frequent and the people who spent the most money are always at the top of the food chain. That is the basic concept". (source: Kurtz, Brian, Overdeliver, USA, Hay House, 2019). An RFM analysis shows commonalities and differences between new and repeat customers and identifies gaps in Louis' customer journey.

What if you're struggling with your customer profile? BRENT's Right Fit Match helps you articulate what you sell and who buys your product. We'll support you in developing your detailed customer profile, focusing on their pain points and the unique solution you provide. From there, we identify opportunities that make buying your product the next logical step for your customer and incorporate their preferences into our automated system so that you have a customer for life.

CHAPTER 16

GDD or Growth Driven Design

The web design model is broken.

The traditional web design model is broken. Typically, most websites are designed by graphic designers who have very little, if any, understanding of what the client's process, services or products really are. They don't recognize who the person coming to the website is, or what they are looking for at the moment that they discover the website. As a result, most websites have a really poor conversion rate. The majority of traffic is coming to a site, looking around, maybe clicking on a few different pages to see what there is to see. Then they leave because there's no compelling reason for them to stay and actually do anything. That is a problem for the business owner because they spent a lot of money having a website or landing page built and those pages aren't converting, because there was no thought given to why their prospective patient, client or customer is coming to the page. What are they looking for? What do they need? How can the business help them?

There is a further problem.

It's not just the owner of the business that gets upset. It's also the designer or the web builder that has issues as well because they're not given all the tools that they need in order to do a good job. The business owner often doesn't fully understand their own process for having a prospective buyer go through their sales process to the point where they become a paying customer. That lack of systemization causes a lot of frustration for the web builder because there's no way for the owner of the business to adequately give the required information to them to make the site function in the conversion of prospects to paying customers. All they can do without the knowledge of a system is to make a pretty site.

Now, fortunately, there is a better way to build sites.

It involves strategically thinking about where the buyer is in the process at the moment that they land on the website and not to try to make one page do all the work. When you think about where a prospect is in their journey, they could be problem unaware, solution unaware or both. This means that not only are they not looking for your solution, they don't even realize they have a problem yet.

An example of that would be a person who is in early stages of cancer. They don't realize they are sick yet as there's no symptoms, they don't feel bad and everything seems to be okay. However, underneath the surface something is going on that they're unaware of and therefore they're not going to be looking for any solution yet. Because they don't yet know they have a problem, this is where you would direct traffic to what is referred to as a cold page where we are educating the prospect about the problem that they may not even know they have. You could, for example, send them to a page telling about an executive or VIP physical so that they could be proactive with their health, finding out where they are now and where they could expect to be in 2, 5, 10 years. That would be an example of a service for someone who is both problem unaware and solution unaware.

From that scenario, you move to where they are problem aware but they are solution unaware. This requires a different conversation to a prospective buyer because they now know they have a problem and are starting to look for solutions to solve it. Using the cancer analogy, they could be looking for a cancer treatment, they could be looking for an oncologist, or maybe they are looking for holistic alternatives to traditional western medicine. They are at a different point in the buying journey now so you need to have a different page for them to go to where your solution is presented in the most favorable way to get them to respond. It needs to answer the questions they will have about what your solution is.

After that level of awareness, your potential buyer is now both problem and solution aware, so now you need to make sure that they are aware of YOUR solution. They are looking at whatever you are offering as a solution and comparing you directly to other service or product providers that are presenting similar services or other solutions to the issue. This is typically where most marketing for small businesses tends to start. Potential buyers are comparing dentists to dentists, or four door sedan to four door sedan. This is the point you need to provide clear reasoning for them to choose you over every other solution, including doing nothing.

Following through their journey, they're at the stage where they are aware of what the problem is, what the solutions are and probably what all their options are. Now a lot of marketing tends to just assume it to be a matter of price. This is typical to a lot of dental or automotive advertising. Dentists often make a point of comparing how much they cost, competing with other practices in their area. Or you see an ad from a car dealer, and the main message of the ad is the price, with the monthly payment, telling you to come in and buy

TODAY. This type of marketing only resonates with someone who has made the decision they're going to buy and now they're just price shopping. This point is very far down in the sales funnel. But doing this kind of marketing, you're not giving yourself any opportunity to differentiate yourself from your competitors in a meaningful way if all you are focusing on is price.

So, knowing the different parts of the funnel you need to address on your website, the best way to build a one that converts is to use data.

How can you do this, I'm sure you are asking. Instead of building a traditional website, built on assumptions with no optimization and using all of your budget upfront, you use a launch pad site. You build in a compressed time frame, you validate your assumptions quickly using data-driven conclusions and then use your budget to optimize your site.

Once the launch pad website is operational, it's key to collect data as quickly as possible. You want to use as many different tools as you can to find out what prospective buyers are clicking on, what they're looking at, what videos they're watching and how much of each video are they watching? When they watch the first video, are they going to the second video? Are they consuming content on video that is short or are they watching something that is long? You should be using a heat map to track movements on each page to see where they're scrolling to and what they're looking at. All of this data is available, some with free tools and more with paid. If you use the data you can very quickly optimize your launch pad website and give your prospective buyers the information that they're looking for. In comparison to the traditional website model of building an entire website and then launching, the launch pad with quick iterations is far more efficient at generating business for you swiftly and it allows you to optimize faster.

Another key component of building a website that converts is having a process of ongoing digital hygiene. Digital hygiene means that your site is going to be updated regularly. This means using the data you collect to remove content that is outdated or not being consumed by your buyers. Be sure that everything is current. Remove bios for staff no longer with you and add new staff quickly. Search engines love it when a site stays 'fresh'. The more you update, the more it encourages bots to 'crawl' and index your site . This makes it much easier for you to rank for search engine optimization, and on your search engine results pages.

One of the most complex parts of building a website that converts as many prospects into buyers as possible is reviewing your analytics regularly. Making sure that your analytics are measuring the key performance indicators that are going to give you the best information is crucial. Use the latest version of Google Analytics. Set up tracking of your UTM parameters (short tags at the end of the web address) whenever you're referring to another page, so that you can keep track of what campaign your leads are coming from, what keywords are being used, and what kind of content people are consuming. Google Analytics is an extraordinarily powerful tool. However, it does require a skilled statistician to look at the data and put it into terms that the average business owner can understand. For Analytics, we recommend hiring a specialist instead of trying to do this yourself.

Interestingly, even though data can give you a lot of insights into what people are doing on your website, the best option to get this information is still to reach out and poll visitors to your website.

This should include prospects, customers, and especially your Tier A customers. These are the people that are going to give you the best feedback on what they do and do not like about your website. Raw data will only take you so far. But going the extra mile and reaching your key clients and prospects, you'll have the opportunity to dig deep into what they're really thinking. One of the things you can do and we highly recommend is that you actually get them to look at a specific page and find out what it is they like and don't like and what questions are not being answered. When they go to your page, what is it that they want to know and what do they do when the information they need is not there? Insights like this will help you increase the conversion rates of your website significantly.

CHAPTER 17
Blog Monetization

The purpose of blogging is to help your clients or potential clients solve their problems while connecting them with you/your business, and your community.

Why Blog?

With blogging you can share your personality and your business through custom content, opinions, and points of interest on a host of topics. Blogging promotes your business, establishes you as a subject matter authority, helps customers get to know you, and warms up prospects by offering them useful information. With newly enforced privacy, it is more important than ever to communicate regularly with your past, present, and future clients; blogs offer a shortcut to communicating directly and regularly with your existing customers.

Blogs that include a call to action or CTA allow new readers to subscribe to your business to build your client base.

In short, blogging can be as effective or more effective at promoting your business than advertising. However, there are a few things to keep in mind when crafting your message for the web.

SEO is Critical

Gone are the days of slapping up an article stuffed with keywords for the sake of having something with SEO on your website. Readers are discerning and don't want to waste their time sifting through detritus to find a kernel of knowledge. They want to be educated, served and engaged. The expectation is for well-written and researched custom content blog posts delivered from your perspective and area of expertise.

Quality content is a great starting place, but it isn't enough. Search engine optimization (SEO) is critical to make your articles and website visible to people searching by keywords associated with your product or service. If your business sells chocolate — you need to research which keywords put your website at the top of search engine results so that people choose your product first over the 150 others. If you're thinking of keyword stuffing, don't, its a no no. Stuffing content with keywords means you have focused on the SEO results and not the reader, which drops the quality of your content and drives readers away. Search engines are also discerning and condemn the practice of keyword stuffing. Filling content with needless keywords can lead to a search penalty and will drop your ratings. Instead, start with quality content and use keywords organically within the content.

Time is money, and if it takes you three hours per blog post or writing is not your thing, consider outsourcing to a writer who can capture your voice and tone.

How to Monetize Your Blog
If you're thinking — "for all that effort, shouldn't a blog post be making me money?" You're right; it should

Always Include a Call to Action (CTA)
After creating search engine optimized quality content, the next step in monetizing your blog is to include a strong call to action or CTA. A CTA leads your readers to a specific action, such as subscribing to

your blog, downloading a report or whitepaper, or filling out a landing page form. Subscribing captures the reader's contact information for your list.

Once you have a list, it is helpful to segment it based on where the customers are in your lifecycle and what tailored content is more relevant to them. Segmenting will help you create CTAs specific to the customer's entry point in the cycle, which will increase your conversion rates. For example, a visitor CTA; "get my free guide now," a lead CTA; "start my free trial now," and an existing customer CTA; "get my download now." Specific CTA's move your visitor, lead, or customer to the next logical step in their buying process.

There is a variety of CTAs you can include in your blog post; some are placed at the end to increase conversion, others are included in the blog text or are linked to additional blog content, and some are placed on the side of the blog. The action you want the visitor to take will determine where the CTA is placed. Additionally, it's good practice to change the wording in your offers to keep things fresh over time. The fundamental CTAs are:

- ## Social Media CTAs

  Effective use of a CTA is to connect your business with social media. If someone likes your business and your content, they'll probably be interested in future content. Your business can post content on social media that readers can follow by creating a CTA in each social media channel. By simply clicking a button, they can follow you.

- ## Blog Subscriptions CTAs

  If readers like your blog posts, they can subscribe to your posts by email, alerting them when you post new content. By filling out a simple form with a name/email address, visitors are added to your subscriber base.

- ## Comment CTAs

Many blogs encourage their readers to share their thoughts and opinions on their articles. Your CTA can say, "share your thoughts about this blog," or you can ask them a question on a specific topic from your blog.

A comment CTA encourages reader interaction and nurtures the relationship.

- ## In-Line CTAs

A call to action doesn't have to be a button; it can also be as simple as a link within your article that provides additional information on a specific topic. The link serves the same purpose as a button by directing people to act.

- ## Sidebar CTAs

These sidebars are great if you have content relevant to your company that is not crucial to your blog post's content. The purpose of sidebar CTAs is to drive your company goals and be seen by anyone viewing the site, not necessarily searching for a blog.

Analysis

Metrics allow you to analyze blog posts and individual pages to see who and how visitors engage with your content. Analytics also provides insights on your sources of website traffic, your search engine optimization, and your website's overall performance. BRENT's structured system provides a granular view of the content-based interactions, including views, submissions, new contacts, customers, average bounce rate, average time on page, exit rate, and entrances. These metrics give your accurate measurements on how your blog post performs, who is engaging, where they're from. These metrics help you to identify gaps and make improvements.

Tip

Two proven techniques to capitalize on the knowledge gained from your highly engaged readers;

- reach out by phone, email, or FedEx to build the connection

- print a summary of your weekly blogs with your blog's anchor image, and send by email or FedEx either once a week, twice a month, or once a month. The higher up the customer is on the pyramid, the more frequent the interaction.

Private Library

Over time, you will have amassed a large collection of blog posts which can be beneficial ongoing information for both you and your customers. Think of these blog posts as your private lending library. You bought or earned the knowledge, you are storing it, and you decide who has access. Like a library, readers appreciate an efficient filing system that makes their search simple and fast. A search field on your website gives readers the option to find specific topics or pages quickly. The search bar encourages your readers to return to your website when they are seeking future information. A positive user experience lends itself to return visits.

Put your knowledge and experience to work in blogs that build relationships, generate leads, and close sales. BRENT's structured system can access keywords through SEO, monetize your blog, segment your CTAs, and include a field search function to make your library of blogs accessible to your new and returning customers.

CHAPTER 18
Sales Pages That Sell

There are five main web pages that allow you to sell from your website. The five pages you absolutely must have are; a cold page, a warm page, the hot page, an offer page and a home page. With these, your website will convert.

Cold Pages

The cold page is a web page that you send traffic to where the prospect is both unaware of the problem and your solution. This is the beginning of the buyer journey. On this page, the purpose is to educate the prospect about the problem and also introduce them to how your product or service can solve that problem. Ideally, there should be something on the cold page that will allow you to collect a name and an email, or other contact information, so that you can continue to communicate with them after this interaction. You want to connect with them regularly, offer more information that explains how their problem could be solved with your product or service and answer questions they have.

Warm Pages

At this point the prospect knows who you are, and is beginning to see you as a trusted source. The warm page will generally get more engagement and starts to position you as an expert trusted source that they can rely on to get answers to their questions. You will be sought out in order to solve whatever problem it is that they're having. Warm pages can typically offer longer content. For example, this might be where you offer a 30 minute or longer recorded webinar, because at this point, they are already seeking the solution that you provide for their problem.

Hot Pages

The hot page is for the prospect that is ready to buy. By the time someone gets to this page, it should be just a question of whether they want to buy your product or service versus another vendor or supplier's solution, or bother doing anything at all. This is where you need to be sure that you're answering all the questions that they possibly have. Make sure that the testimonials that are on the page are relevant to the thought process that got them to the page in the first place. Everything on the hot page needs to be congruent, meaning the entire page is written in a way that finishes the narrative that is playing in their mind so that they see your product or service as the solution to the problem that they are experiencing. If you answer all the objections that they could possibly have, you position yourself as being the only logical choice. The hot page truly is where the rubber meets the road.

Creating Your Cold, Warm, and Hot Pages

Cold, Warm and Hot pages are constructed similarly, the differences being the copy and images or videos. The essential elements are:

1. Each page has a header banner that contains your logo and some way for the viewer to respond NOW—typically a phone number with instructions on how to claim the next action you want them to take. For example 800-555-1212 with "Call Now To Book Your Free Assessment" immediately underneath.

2. Ideally, you begin with a short, punchy "pre-header" above the actual headline. The preheader is either used to frame the ideal reader for the page OR to give credibility to the writer. Examples include "A special message to busy Moms that just can't get enough time to go to the gym..." or "Indian immigrant turned Marketing Guru reveals his entire marketing plan..."

3. The main headline conveys the main benefit or value proposition you are offering your customers, clients, or patients. Professional copywriters will often invest hours writing dozens (The top "A" copywriters will always write 100+) of headlines. They know that a strong, "killer" headline will make the difference between a poor or mediocre response and a wildly successful, profitable response. In all cases, you absolutely must split test your headlines to ensure you're getting maximum profit from each page.

4. Next, immediately below the headline, the page is split into 2 columns with the left column using 2/3 of the page and the right column using 1/3 of the page.

5. At the top of the left column is your sub-headline. The sub-headline supports the headline and proves context to the headline. A well-crafted sub-headline solidifies the attention of the viewer and creates sufficient interest in the minds of the page visitors so that they want to consume more of the information on the page.

6. Below the sub-headline is an image or video that is relevant to the messaging and attracts the interest of the viewer.

7. Immediately below the image or video is copy that expands on the promise/offer/value proposition you laid out in your headline.

8. Now it's time to use copy to get the viewer to take the desired action. Copy should be broken up into short paragraphs for easy reading and should be relevant to the "temperature" of the viewer. All your copy should clearly and concisely describe how you're different from the competition and the value/benefits customers/clients/patients get by using your service(s).

9. Use bullet points or numbered lists to break up copy and highlight the most important benefit/value statements.

10. Close with more copy that again is broken up into short paragraphs for easy reading. The closing copy should also clearly and concisely describe how you're different from the competition as well as detailing the value/benefits customers/clients/patients get by using your service(s).

11. The right side column should have a highly visible CALL TO ACTION FORM at the top. The form will typically have a different colored background to make it "pop" on the page. Copy for the form should utilize with benefit focused lead-ins before the form fields. On the "cold" page, it is generally best to limit the information you request to first name and email address. Asking for too much information on the "cold" page will often significantly lower the number of viewers willing to "opt-in" and get the information or lead magnet you're offering. You can usually ask for additional information like last name and possibly the viewers phone number on the "warm" page. Viewers of the "hot" page will often be willing to give substantially more information including years in business, the viewer's position in a company, or even annual income as they're already more likely to be considering your product or service solution.

12. Every form should have an Action Oriented Button. Never use "Submit" on an action button. Instead, use a phrase like "Click To Get Your Free Report" or "Click To Schedule A Complimentary Discovery Call".

13. The bottom portion of the right side column under the Call To action form is your "Proof Zone". Use testimonials, client logos, media reprints or quotes to build trust and authority.

14. Below the columns, revert back to a single, full width column and add another Call to Action. Follow the Call to Action with copy to reinforce your call to action for the page. You can include your phone number again. Remind people to fill out the form or do whatever it is that you want them to do on this page. Just make sure you convey again the benefit they'll receive for taking action.

15. The last element on the page is the footer. A typical footer layout is HOME | CONTACT | ABOUT | PRIVACY POLICY | TERMS OF SERVICE. This should be the ONLY navigation links off the page. Check with your media provider as these links are often required in their terms of service and forgetting (or excluding) these links can cause your traffic driving ads to be rejected or worse, have your ad account rescinded.

Offer Pages

The offer page is where you present your offer and give the prospect the opportunity to take up your call to action, whatever that may be. This could mean that they are going to make a purchase, schedule a discovery call or RSVP to an event.

Often, your Offer Page should mimic the look of the cold, arm, and hot pages. This is because prospects can become confused when they are presented with a dramatically different page design or layout. This can cause confusion in the mind of the prospect leading them to ask "Am I on the right page?" This will almost ALWAYS kill a sale and must be avoided.

Instead, use a layout similar to the pages they've seen before but give them all the reasons that they need to take action right now. Clearly state the steps that they need to take to consummate a successful transaction with your business. Amp up your offer page and make a stronger case by stacking additional offers.

"If you take action A now, you will not only get product or service X, you'll also get Y and Z."

Bonuses, premiums, and special offers are essential to converting as many prospects as possible from the offer page. Additionally, upon a successful transaction, offer either an upsell or a down sell that is congruent with the purchase just made. For example, if you are offering a home study course, your upsell might be, "Are you concerned that you may not have the time to do this yourself? Why not let us do it for you?" This kind of an upsell is extremely effective when presented properly, because it gives the prospective buyer the opportunity to get better results, faster. This is a very lucrative strategy for many businesses. Alternatively, if your prospect doesn't take the original offer or the upsell, you should offer a downsell. Ultimately, the series of offers, upsells and downsells are going to be dependent on your business and what the testing tells you is most effective.

Home Pages

On your website, the homepage is a catch all page. Generally speaking, you should NEVER drive paid traffic to a home page. Home pages are designed for prospects that find your company either through referral or search. They are critical to have because someone who comes to you as a referral or by searching for you is looking for very different Information than the information you would present to them on a sales page. It is essential that you immediately start by giving value and building rapport.

Your home page is the first step in what will hopefully be a long relationship. But in much the same way that you would never go on a first date and ask for their hand in marriage before getting to know them; you use your homepage to introduce yourself to your reader. Give them an idea of who you are and what you do. You want to encourage them to start an exchange of information with you so that you can begin to understand who your prospect is, who you're talking to and what they need. One of the ways that works very well for doing this is to have them take a short quiz which will present them with the information that they would find most beneficial in dealing with your products and services.

A component we recommend on every home page is an "exit pop". Exit pops are windows that "pop up" on the viewers screen when we detect the views intent to leave the page. For example, if the view moves their mouse to the "back" button, this would signify their intent to leave the page and would trigger the "pop". This is your last chance to collect your viewers' name and information so make sure you're offering something that is particularly appealing.

CHAPTER 19
Strategy of Strategies

Is a large portion of your marketing focused on your digital presence? With most businesses, the answer is a resounding yes! Since online businesses are always striving to grow their presence, wouldn't it make sense to develop a digital strategy that fuels sales by converting visitors into loyal customers?

To help you understand and improve your digital presence, I've put together this chapter which will cover four sections;

1. Digital Marketing Strategy

2. SMART Growth Goals

3. Customer Acquisition

4. Master Strategy Model

Digital Marketing Strategy

A digital marketing strategy involves a sequence of activities you take that use digital platforms to achieve your goals. Digital platforms include Facebook, Google, YouTube, Twitter, Instagram, Pinterest, Snapchat, and LinkedIn.

It's important to remember that digital marketing encompasses everything digital or, more simply, 5Ds, including digital technology, digital platforms, digital devices, digital media, and digital data.

Within the digital marketing sphere, you can market on three channels, paid, owned, and earned media. A paid channel is any channel you pay to advertise, such as Google AdWords, social media, or sponsored posts/websites. Earned media refers to advertising that is done for you through word of mouth, and an owned channel includes your digital assets such as your website and blogs, social media profile, or images.

Your business has its own digital fingerprint, which means that your digital strategy will most likely involve several approaches or a combination of approaches.

A strong digital marketing strategy incorporates three-time frames:

- Short — 1 year
- Medium- 2 years
- Long — 3 + years

SMART Goals

Setting goals within multiple time frames allows you to set Specific, Measurable, Attainable, Realistic, and Timely (SMART) goals for each stage and age of your marketing journey. Not to be confused with your digital strategy, your digital campaign helps you achieve your short, medium, and long-term goals. But successfully charting your internet campaigns requires a digital marketing strategy.

How to create a digital marketing strategy

I've written about the steps in previous chapters; however, they bear repeating to illustrate how they function within the overall digital strategy. The first step you are already familiar with:

1. **Create your customer persona**
   Knowing who to target is key. It's critical you understand your

customers wants, needs, and pain points. Having a persona or personas allows you to tailor your strategy to them. Specific is terrific, and the more granular your data, the better your persona. Location, income, age, employment, gender, goals, interests, and pain points help you form your persona. A robust persona shapes your digital strategy and supports you in understanding which channels to market to specific personas.

2. **Set time frames for your goals**

   While setting your short, medium, and long-term goals, be sure to align them with your business goals, as your strategic digital marketing goals should support your overarching goals. Undefined goals without timeframes never get done. Make sure you have defined what you want to accomplish when you want to accomplish the goal and what tool you will use to measure the accomplishment—SMART goals. Metrics provide a brutally honest yardstick of what is and isn't working and can measure views, bounce, and open rates.

3. **Assess your online digital marketing strategies**

   As part of ongoing improvement, it's important to review your earned, owned, and paid media metrics. Are people visiting your website? Are they reading the articles? Where are your traffic coming leads coming from? Which media provides the best and most consistent results? Which provides the worst results? Are your customers engaging on your social media platforms? Are your pay-per-click ads generating leads? If so, how many? Do they convert to sales? Making a continual assessment of your digital marketing efforts will help you understand what is and isn't working within each campaign.

4. **Set a budget for each campaign**

   Knowing what you can spend on each campaign will help

you make the most of your marketing dollars and stop you from overspending. Remember to budget in your resources, including the number of people, the time needed, and the tools required for each campaign.

The idea of following these four steps in the digital marketing strategy is to see what is and isn't working, identify gaps, and continually modify your strategy until you reach your goals. The next step in a digital strategy is to create a sustainable method of bringing in new customers.

Customer Acquisition

New customers are the driving force of any business. New customers keep a business growing and thriving. The tricky part is understanding and targeting your marketing effectively in each step of the buyer process and then creating a sustainable customer acquisition strategy that is flexible enough to evolve with the times.

Buyer's Journey

To understand the customer journey, it's necessary to identify the customer's buying process stages. Customers follow a four-step process, and acquiring customers within the buyer's journey requires specific strategies for each of the four steps;

1. Awareness. In this stage, the customer is
   made aware of your product or service.

2. Interest. In the second step, potential customers may
   be spending more time on your website, and they
   may have downloaded a free product or two.

3. Decision. At this step, the customer has
   decided to buy your product.

4. Action. In the final step, the customer takes
    action and buys your product or service.

There are multiple methods of acquiring new customers, including targeted content marketing, SEO, blogging, videos, free content offers such as eBooks, whitepapers, reports, social media, and email marketing. Choosing the best channels to acquire new customers depends on many factors, including your audience, resources, and game plan. Whichever channel you choose, for it to be effective, it must be relevant to your audience and include a call-to-action.

During the process, your sales team will identify whether the prospect falls into either the marketing qualified lead (MQL) or the sales qualified lead (SQL). Typically, MQL's have a good chance of turning into paying customers; however, they need more nurturing to move them up the next step in the buying process, whereas SQL's are considered ready to buy and need a final push to move into action.

A first-time visitor who downloaded one form is an MQL. A visitor who has frequented your site numerous times and downloaded a few pieces of content may be an SQL. A visitor who has requested a phone call or meeting is an SQL.

Customer Acquisition Cost (CAC)

As you well know, there's a cost to acquiring new customers. Expenses or costs of marketing can include many expenses such as money spent for advertising, employee salaries, content creation, the technology used by your marketing and sales teams, production costs for creating physical products such as a camera for videos, and maintaining inventory such as software updates.

There is a neat little formula for calculating the customer acquisition cost called CAC (the acronym). The lower the CAC, the higher the profit, the higher the CAC, the lower the profit. To calculate your CAC, choose the month, quarter, or year, add your total marketing and sales expenses and divide the total sum by the number of new customer acquisitions during that time frame. That number is your cost of acquiring a new customer. Determining the CAC reveals marketing, campaign, and sales insights.

CAC = (cost of sales + cost of marketing)

New Customers Acquired

For example, if your customer service team has managed to keep your customers happy, and they spread the word through reviews and testimonials and referring family and friends, the CAC is low, and your profits are high because your loyal customers are bringing in new customers free of charge to you.

If your social media ads are costing you huge dollars but only bring in a trickle of leads, your CAC is high and the profit low. In this case, you will need to reassess to lower its CAC or eliminate it from your marketing strategy.

Customer Lifetime Value (CLV)

[sometimes called Lifetime Customer Value]

Another valuable metric to factor into customer acquisition is a customer lifetime value or CLV. CLV predicts the revenue a customer will produce over the lifetime of their relationship with your business. There are four components of CLV; each has a formula, which includes:

- average purchase value; total revenue/# of purchases (within the same time period)

- average purchase frequency; # of purchases/# of customers (within the same time period)

- customer value; average purchase value x average purchase frequency

- average customer lifespan; average # of years customer buys from your business

- CLV; customer value x average customer lifespan = amount average customer generates during the course of their relationship with your business

CAC to CLV Ratio

Now that you have your CLV and CAC, it's time to calculate the ratio to reveal customer worth compared to your expenses in acquiring customers CAC:CLV. It would help if you were aiming for a customer value ratio three times higher than your cost of acquiring them or 3:1. Of course, the higher the item, the longer it will take and the higher the CAC cost. A customer buying a $1,000,000 crane will take considerably more time and effort to acquire than a customer buying cosmetic brushes for $60.

Master Strategy Model

Strategies to improve customer acquisition

To bring your CAC:CLV ratio down, and increase your profits, here are a few effective strategies.

- Conversion rate optimization (CRO). Automated submissions and shopping accessible 24/7

- Targeted value. Give customers content, products, services that are valuable to them

- Customer referral program. Free customers — through automated referral systems

- Automated tools/processes to streamline your sales process

- Add more value for your existing customers, and provide appreciation gifts

- Break your business growth into six areas of growth and score each of them from 1 (lowest) to 5 (highest) Acquisition

    1. Awareness   4. Revenue

    2. Acquisition   5. Retention

    3. Active Sales   6. Referrals

- Review the six areas of growth quarterly so that you and your team can identify what or who is performing and what isn't, from there; you can adjust to achieve your goals

- Prioritize three areas at a time focusing on the right activities that move you to the next level of growth

- Set quarterly goals

- Track your metrics

Putting it all together

I've covered a lot of information here, so I'd like to provide a quick summary.

- Before implementing your digital marketing strategy, set short, medium, and long-term goals

- Create a marketing strategy by following four steps; develop customer persona, set timelines, assess strategies, set a budget

- Customer acquisition involves an understanding of the customer buying process and formulas to calculate the CAC, CLV, and CAC:CLV ratio

- Identify the six areas of growth, score them, and review quarterly until goals are achieved

As you can see, setting up a digital marketing strategy is an involved and complex process that requires a solid understanding of your customers, their behaviour, their needs, your sales process, and finally creating mapping a marketing plan template to identify goals and stay on track. A digital marketing strategy is also a crucial component of your business growth.

BRENT's system involves a master strategy model template that provides an efficient format to map your digital marketing strategy. BRENT's template takes you through your marketing strategy, budget, channels, and metrics step by step. BRENT's automated system supports acquiring the right customers and lets them know you value and appreciate them once they've bought your product/service. Utilizing BRENT's powerful marketing tools aligns you with the most current digital initiatives that optimize and automate your processes to drive long-term success.

.

CHAPTER 20
Copy and Content

This is NOT the job for the CEO, CMO or other internal staff

This may actually come as a surprise, but it is not the job of any of the internal employees to write sales copy for a website, a brochure, sales letter, or even a postcard. Sales copy is written from a position of persuasion. Typically, employees tend to write sales copy from the perspective of features and sometimes, if you're lucky, benefits. The simple truth is nobody buys features. You can say that it is made of titanium, that it has eight cylinders, that it's medical grade stainless steel, or that you have a complete law library on site, but the simple truth is none of this matters to a prospect. Now, if you decide to go a little deeper and say what the benefit of those things are. This is better, but it's still not good. The problem is that someone who works for your business is probably trained in your industry, not writing. They are probably not trained in copywriting. Writers not trained in this specific style almost always default to writing about only features and benefits. If the goal is to sell more of your product or service, you definitely do not want to have this kind of copy being produced for your business.

Use professional copywriters

The simple truth is copywriting is an art. It is the marriage of a prospect's desires with the features and benefits of your solution, using persuasive copy that is designed and engineered to get the prospect to take the actions that you as a business owner want them to take. It's essential that this is done in the right sequence. When a piece of copy is improperly structured, you end up having the prospect jumping to conclusions or making assumptions that may not be correct nor get them to take the actions you want. Professional copywriters know this and they're trained to walk your prospect along the path, building up trust, giving them reasons to act, answering questions that they may not even know they have. This is done in a way that is engaging without being pushy. Proper content creation builds trust and positions a prospect to not only buy your product or service, but also to become engaged with your company, making them more likely to buy again as well as to refer.

Use internal staff to strategize with external writers

The brand CMO and director of marketing should participate in copy-strategy conversations and work with professional, EXTERNAL copywriter(s) and content producers to do the writing. Do not just assume the writer can do the job without guidance. They will need input and you should always have a hand in to make sure your message is correct.

Strategy of Strategies

The highest level marketing begins with a strategy of strategies. While this may sound slightly confusing, a strategy of strategies takes individual initiatives that you may have within the company ensures that they are all married together so that they work with synchronicity. For example, if you have a Mother's Day promotion, then logically that Mother's Day promotion would end once Mother's Day occurs. When you're using a strategy and strategies, you are thinking about the next promotion. And the one after that, and the one after that. Every strategy handshakes with proceeding and the following strategy. But again, this comes back to marketing congruency, where everything seems to flow naturally, especially from the perspective of the prospect. All marketing strategies are planned in advance on a marketing calendar. This allows you to not only make sure that every strategy flows from one to the other, but it also allows you to repeat the calendar yearly, making investments with ongoing improvements. You are always able to optimize each of the campaigns that you were running at any one given time.

Management needs to work with the copywriting team to create a marketing calendar that has an overarching, or parent, strategy with sub, or baby, strategies, working seamlessly underneath it. It's important not to underestimate the difficulty in putting all these pieces together and it is essential that you have an effective coach to help you put all of the strategies together in a way that ensures success.

PART 4

Hi, I am **BRENT**
eLaunchers
eLaunchers.com

The Journey
Forward

CHAPTER 21

Everyone Needs an Elephant

Congratulations. You're almost done reading this book. I hope you're convinced an automated marketing and sales platform to help attract visitors, convert leads, and close customers is a must-have for your business.

I hope I have inspired you to think carefully about your customer persona, and customer journey, and their underlying problem that you can help them resolve.

I wrote this book to be the beginning of our customer relationship, and as I see it, you have three options available.

1. You can shut this book and never look at it again or do anything with the information I shared. I genuinely hope you are not considering this option.

2. You can take the information I gave you from this book and learn how to leverage the techniques and strategies I outlined.

3. You can make the sensible decision to schedule a consultation session with me to discuss your business needs. I make scheduling easy, and there is no cost or obligation to you, so what have you got to lose? We may work together; we may not; either way, I'm hoping I have helped you on your path to prosperity. Visit _____

As you've seen, BRENT can combine various functions that allow your marketing and sales activities to be managed all in one place. Within weeks, with BRENT's platform, eLaunchers.com can turnkey the implementation and automation of your sales and marketing processes.

Since we are systems people, we have standard operating procedures (SOPs) for everything. We have systematized the BRENT Platform's implementation to a pre-populated project management template with implementation tasks and copywriting tasks.

You might say, 'But my business is different. What if it doesn't fit the pre-populated project template?' And if you say so… you would be right. Your business IS different, and all the copy and graphics work will fit your context, concepts, and marketing modality. What BRENT offers is a system that provides a default road map. The same system has already taken dozens of companies from Frankensoft to a seamlessly integrated and automated sales and marketing process.

Our team will set up the command & control center and the communications processes to implement your minimal pain plan. Our process gets things done fast and right the first time, staying on time and budget. Most importantly, the implementation plan brings an order, discipline, and customer-focused workflow to your inbound marketing, sales, and customer service.

Our system is set up in three process phases:

Phase I, Planning

This process usually takes anywhere from 1-12 days. Within that time, we define your business concepts and marketing strategy and complete your 73-point business-building checklist. From this information, we compile your 2-page marketing plan and plan your 3-5-year marketing roadmap, with annual priorities and quarterly Specific, Measurable, Attainable, Relevant, and Time-Bound (SMART) goals.

Phase II, Design & Build

Magic happens in this phase. We design your systems and processes for your website, blog, funnels, landing pages, and call to action through our marketing automation platform.

Phase III, Deliver & Execute

In this phase, we deliver your online and offline marketing campaigns, document the findings, and assess which conversion methods work best for your business. We've discovered clients are all different. Some want inspirational articles with lots of images, others like to see comparisons from charts and graphs, and a third might only respond if you tug on their heartstrings. Documentation and trending help analyze what's working best for your business.

BRENT is your elephant that outfits your business with the right processes and systems to take your prospects on a three-phase journey. The end goal is to turn attraction into prospects that become leads, which convert into lifelong customers. If that sounds like something you'd like for your business, I'd like to help.

If I can be of service to you, I'd like to know-how.

Best wishes as you follow your journey to success.

Parthiv Shah
pshah@elaunchers.com
301.760.4940

BONUS

Marketing Automation

by Dan Kennedy

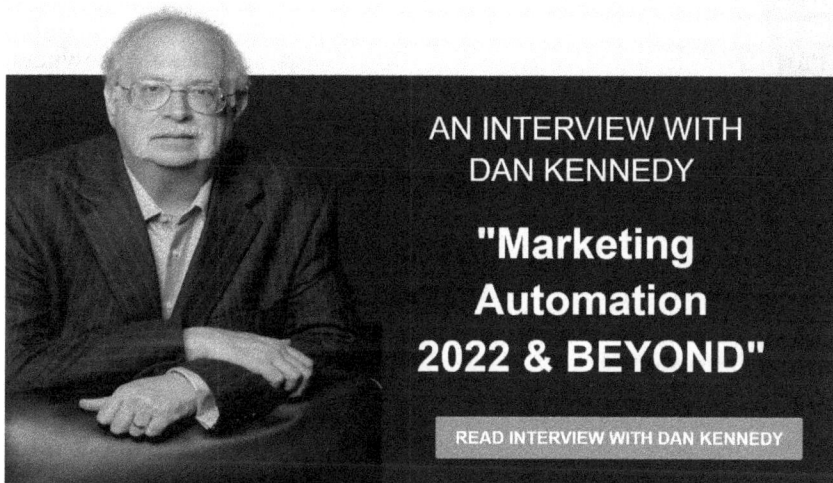

AN INTERVIEW WITH
DAN KENNEDY

**"Marketing
Automation
2022 & BEYOND"**

READ INTERVIEW WITH DAN KENNEDY

Parthiv: I'm getting an opportunity to ask Dan Kennedy some questions about "tech", about automation, a subject many people might think an odd fit for him—but I can assure you that he is familiar, engaged, and has definitive viewpoints and advice. I'm not going to take time to recite Dan's biography or resume, you are probably familiar. He is in his 5th decade of being paid kings' ransoms for his strategic advice about marketing. Dan, I have questions... questions I don't think you've been asked by others...

DAN: Well, let's hope I have answers.

Parthiv: Why have you pushed your clients and business owners following you to Marketing Automation?

DAN: I lived and built businesses when dinosaurs roamed. We did everything via manual labor, so marketing, both front-end, for lead production and customer acquisition, and for follow-up, after missed sales opportunities or after first purchase, was severely constrained. It was slow, expensive, difficult, and it required enormous discipline and determination to do it. At one point, I was running a company where we were doing large quantity multi-step direct-mail, with list segmentation, using 33-up Avery® mailing label sheets, done on an IBM typewriter, put in tickler files. A client had a computer database program and a multi-step trigger system for follow-up he had gotten built from scratch for his company, and he generously sent his nerd over to install it for us. It was primitive by today's standards, but it was rocket science then, and it changed a lot. Fewer people doing clumsy things, speed, more capability equaled doing more, lower costs. Note the "fewer people". We literally doubled the value of every lead. Later, when my company became Glazer-Kennedy®, the database management, the marketing implementation became much better and more sophisticated, with better tools—but it was still cumbersome and difficult, and as bad or worse, it was something we could do but many of our member-businesses could not "model" and use.

Parthiv: So, about that time, you were a founding investor and supporter of Infusionsoft, now Keap®. Why?

DAN: The members of my Inner Circle — now living as MagneticMarketing.com — were actually "stuck" like I had been stuck, although in a much more advanced place. I provided them with very smart, very effective, very comprehensive direct marketing strategies for any business, A to Z, small or bigger, and they understood them and wanted to do them — but most were stymied and frustrated by the implementation. As a practical matter, the small business had to add staff, use several different software products that wouldn't communicate (interface) with each other so manual bridging was necessary and errors occurred, good data was hard to come by, and it was just too much for the butcher, baker, candlestick-maker, chiropractor, lawyer, independent salesman to bear. And I had no good solutions to offer. Clate Mask literally built the original Infusionsoft to fix all this — as we said then, to conquer the chaos, integrate all marketing, and get things done. Years have passed since then, and Infusionsoft, now Kaep, has had evolutionary and revolutionary changes, as has the entire field of Marketing Automation.

Parthiv: What is your current thinking about Marketing Automation?

DAN: <u>First, it has new, extra essentiality.</u> The Pandora's Box of media; online media available, to use and manage...the labor shortage and wage inflation...the expectations of customers — the way they judge a business by response time...the heightened competition and the new currency of attention and interest...all require doing a lot more, but the business owner has to do all that with less; less staff, less overhead, less difficulty. That makes getting the right Marketing Automation functioning for a business vital.

<u>Second, as an investor, I see the field as being very strong, because of what I just said</u>. As you know, I am a shareholder in Kaep, and I am enthused about the recent developments there — Clate re-taking the reins, the software products being greatly improved, and the return of many "lost" prior users. I own stock in Hubspot. And in a couple small, fledgling start-ups in this field. I missed investing in Salesforce.com at a reasonable entry price, which I regret. I am now associated with ClickFunnels and Russell Brunson. Russell is a long-time "fan" and user of my strategies, and he recently acquired the NO B.S./ Magnetic Marketing business. I have clients in the field, notably you and your eLaunchers.com, and I've witnessed and hopefully helped you grow your company and strengthen its capabilities for clients who want to delegate their Marketing Automation implementation. You, of course, make use of all these tools and platforms differently for different clients and situations; Kaep, ClickFunnels, Hubspot. Somewhat like a doctor chooses and mixes and matches different medicines, surgeries, non-surgical treatments for a particular patient.

<u>Third, I am currently advising my Private Clients to cut their staff size, to *reduce* their staff cost as percentage of gross, to be leaner 'n meaner than ever, without compromising their success</u>. There are many reasons for this I don't have to drill down on here, like labor shortages, the quality issues, the new "woke-ism" infecting workplaces and putting employers in peril, a federal government disregard for and disapproval of employer rights, and more. Now, given the labor shortages, competition for staff, and wage inflation, this advice I'm giving carries with it a great deal of difficulty. It requires making

significant changes in a business. One is that automation has to be accelerated, expanded and utilized to replace people, and that can be done with marketing.Last, I'll make the point that the costs of lead production and of new customer acquisition are rich in inflation. Everything about it costs more and will keep costing more. This mandates a tough-minded zero tolerance policy for waste or loss. This screams for comprehensive Marketing Automation, because it performs its programmed tasks perfectly, without fail, without forgetting, without mood swings, without procrastination, nothing falling through a crack. If a business employs sales professionals, on the phone, in physical locations, it is vital not to waste their time or talent, now, at all. This means using Automated Marketing to replace cold prospecting and to better pre-qualify and pre-sell prospects in advance of the interaction with the salesperson, and to have a very robust follow-up system, automated, for the Appointment, No Sale prospects. This can allow reduction of the number of salespeople, keeping the best, discarding the mediocre, while simultaneously INCREASING sales and possibly increasing price elasticity and profitability.

This concept of mine — *more, from fewer and less* — is the subject of one of my most recent books, ALMOST ALCHEMY. Candidly, I did not say enough in it about this, about Marketing Automation. Just 2 years ago, the need was not as acute. But it does examine all the places inside a business where losses occur, like losses of lead or customer value. It reveals all the holes to be corked. Many can best be corked with Marketing Automation.

Parthiv: What about the cost?

DAN: Essentially, the business owner is paying for an Automated Marketing System whether he has one, has a good one, or not. He is either invested in it and getting a return on that investment that can be measured, in deriving improved value from his ad spend, marketing spend, leads, customers, employed salespeople — or — he is suffering losses, some known, some unknown, in poorer than necessary ROI on those things. And that may have been tolerable a few years ago, but not now. In fact, it is very unlikely we escape some form of a recession in the near future. Today's rising, persistent inflation has recession as its only known cure. Businesses not fully weaponized to withstand a recession, in part by maximizing value of every lead, every sales opportunity and every customer, and in part by being as financially efficient as possible, can be wiped out.

Parthiv: Closing comments?

DAN: My late speaking colleague and friend Zg Ziglar used to say people needed a periodic "check-up from the neck up". He was talking about mind-set, attitude and personal philosophy. I can say the same thing about a business' marketing and, with it, the extent and soundness of the automation of that marketing — it is the business' brain in a way, and it needs a periodic examination, X-rays, MRI's, blood tests; a check-up. The business owner needs to stop running long enough to do this as a critical self-exam, and my book ALMOST ALCHEMY can help. He may need; he probably needs to get a qualified 2nd-opinion, too. An exam by somebody with unbiased eyes and a complete knowledge of what automation is possible in the situation, to maximize positive results. I am NOT a fan of tech for tech's sake. We have to be careful of Drucker's warning about efficiencies at expense or sacrifice of effectiveness. We have to be wary of the magnetism of popular fad-ism; what everybody else is doing. On the other hand, we have to be as smart as we can be. I have a Private Client, Richard James, who consults with solo-practice law firms, who says that systems should run a business and its owner and staff should run the systems. He's right. And we can go a step farther and say, when possible, the systems should run themselves. Great marketing is no better than lousy marketing if it can't be implemented, won't be implemented, can't or won't be implemented with consistency and constancy.

Parthiv: Thank you, Dan, for your time, for this interview. ■

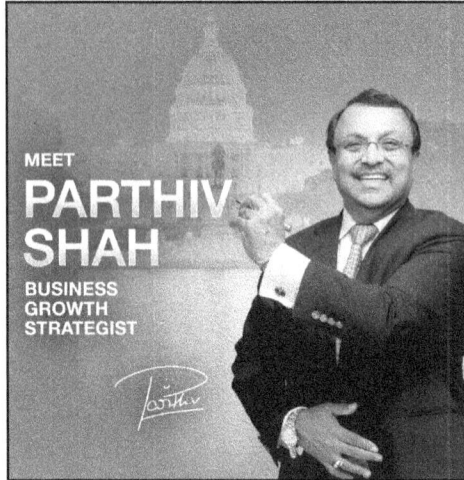

MEET
PARTHIV SHAH
BUSINESS GROWTH STRATEGIST

Book time with Parthiv at
www.meetparthiv.com
and claim your gifts.

Helpful Technology Resources

This is a partial list of technologies I use and recommend. For a complete list, please visit the book website BRENTneverforgets.com/technologies. Please remember, the technologies I am recommending are my current opinion of my preferences at the time of the recommendation and may change or evolve over time. If you are using alternative technologies, that's your call. We all have our favorites. If you do become my private client, we will be using technologies of my choice because they are what our team is trained on, and we know how to support them.

- Inbound marketing and sales: HubSpot

- Cloud based customer experience automation: HubSpot

- CRM System: Email marketing and sales automation platform: HubSpot, Keap

- Website and sales funnel builder: ClickFunnels, WordPress, HubSpot

- Graphic design: Adobe Indesign, Illustrator, Photoshop, Microsoft Publisher

- Web Hosting: WP Engine

- Landing pages: Keap, HubSpot, ClickFunnels

- Website design CMS: HubSpot, WordPress

- Membership sites: Customerhub, Imember360, Wordpress Wishlist

- Social media integration with Keap: Zapier, and HubSpot to Keap native integration

- PCI Compliance and ecommerce credit card processing: Authorize.net, Quickbooks Online

- Video editing : Adobe Premier

- Cloud Computing: Microsoft Office 365

- Online Calendar and Appointment Scheduling: HubSpot, Keap, Calendly

- Cloud file storage: Dropbox, Box, OneDrive, Adobe Creative Cloud

- Note-taking: Microsoft OneNote

- Mobile technology for the road: Latest Samsung phone with S-pen, Microsoft Surface, Microsoft Pen

- Project management and team collaboration: https://monday.com

- Email marketing (small budget or free tools): HubSpot, Keap

- Copywriting: No tune can replace a good copywriter. A machine can not do a Human's job. Skip the AI.

- Text messaging: Yetitext, Justcall, www.fixyourfunnel.com

- List research: www.srds.com (If you need help with list research please book time with me at www.meetparthiv.com)

- Data intelligence and data cleansing: Bulkmailer by Satori, Windowbook, Oracle for database programming

- Online data storage: MySQL

- Preferred programming language: PhP

- Online meeting: Zoom.com

- Reporting and analysis tools: Google Analytics, Infusionsoft Analytics, HubSpot CMS, Databox.com

With evolving technologies, this list becomes obsolete fast. If you are working to refresh or calibrate your Marketing Technologies Deck, I am here to help you understand your options and help you choose the most appropriate technology suite that is good for you. Just book a call with me at www.meetparthiv.com

Frequently Asked Questions

I am frequently asked the same questions from business owners interested in automating their sales and marketing processes, so I wanted to include some of those questions to help you understand how we can work together.

Q Who are eLaunchers?

A. eLaunchers is a turnkey marketing communication firm that offers data-centric automated marketing that integrates email, social media, online marketing, offline marketing, and telephone marketing. BRENT's system creates lead generation, lead capture, and lead conversion from one central location.

It drives prospects to a squeeze page on the homepage, a campaign-specific-URL, or a personalized URL.

It coaxes a prospect to leave their name, email, and phone number, captures and stores their information, and builds a sales funnel that nurtures leads into lifelong customers. The sales funnel can lead up to an initial appointment or a long- term nurture program.

Q Who is your ideal client?

A. Our ideal clients are professionals who realize the importance of having an efficient, automated sales funnel that creates lead generation, lead capture, and lead conversion. Typically, I work well with companies that are already spending money on marketing but are unhappy with the results.

The process we build inserts data markers in your current marketing materials that helps you determine what is and isn't working. That way, you can go in and figure out what to do to turn on the heat or what to tone down or turn off.

Q How do I know your system works?

A. I've been in direct marketing since 1989 and have helped small to not-so-small businesses and organizations compete and win against rivals with colossal marketing dollars.

Since 2002 I've been helping entrepreneurs and business owners build and automate their marketing campaigns by leveraging technology. I have a long and fruitful track record (19 years and counting) of supporting business owners in my community. My clients range from well-known, high-profile direct marketers to local dentists and chiropractors, among many other professionals. We have mailed over a billion pieces of direct mail, produced over 10,000 marketing campaigns, built over 1000 websites and landing pages, and generated over 1,000,000 Personalised URLs (PURLS).

During my MBA, I learned how to utilize the SWOT analysis method, analyzing your business' strengths, weaknesses, opportunities, and treats. It is a handy tool to address what works, what doesn't work, what is missing, how to minimize risks, and how to take the best advantage of success opportunities.

My process builds trust with prospects that then develops into life-long client relationships that can be monitored, measured, and monetized. For real life case studies, check out my eLaunchers

Testimonials and Case Studies https://www.magcloud.com/browse/issue/55600.

Q What is involved in setting up this system?

A. It is a significant relationship that involves substantial time and attention from both of us. As mentioned in Chapter 14, it involves a three-step process.

Phase I, Planning

This process usually takes anywhere from 1-12 days. Within that time, we define your business concepts and marketing strategy and complete your 73-point business-building checklist. From this information, we compile your 2-page marketing plan and plan your 3-5-year marketing roadmap, with annual priorities and quarterly Specific, Measurable, Attainable, Relevant, and Time-Bound (SMART) goals.

Phase II, Design & Build

Magic happens here. We design your systems and processes for your website, blog, funnels, landing pages, and call to action through our marketing automation platform.

Phase III, Deliver and Execute

In this phase, we deliver your online and offline marketing campaigns, document the findings, and assess which conversion methods work best for your business. We've discovered clients are all different. Some want inspirational articles with lots of images, others like to see comparisons from charts and graphs, and a third might only respond if you tug on their heartstrings. Documentation and trending help analyze what's working best for your business.

BRENT outfits your business with the right processes and systems to take your prospects on the three-phase journey. The end goal is to turn attraction into prospects that become leads, which convert into lifelong customers.

Q Do you have a payment plan?

A We have three plans for you to choose from:

1. Initial consultation fee for a day of consult plus year long advisory services

2. One time system building and setup fee with an optional small monthly agency retainer

3. No upfront system building and set up fee and an appropriately priced monthly retainer

With both the system payment methods, all work to implement your fully automated system will be completed by the end of the 12 month period. The only difference is that with the 2nd payment method, you are in control of the amount you would like to pay monthly and the speed and amount of work you would like to have accomplished each month. We do whatever it takes to make you win.

All my services come with a 100% money-back guarantee. We do not guarantee success, and to be honest, I don't always achieve success. I don't have a silver bullet. What I do ensure is that if you are unhappy, that you do request a refund for any fees paid in the last 30 days. If that happens, I am perfectly willing to write off my losses and move on rather than lose a friend.

Q Why do you have a monthly maintenance fee?

A. If you have the ability to manage a complex marketing machine, whether in-house or outsourced, with many moving parts, you won't be in need of our monthly maintenance and therefore there will be no fee. However, if this is not your skill set, or you would rather focus on building your business, you will require us to do that work for you.

I have teams across most time zones in the USA and Canada, as well as other countries. This allows me to deploy your marketing system 24/7. If you're driving home from work and you decide to call me to say, "I want to change campaign number 23 to list segment 6 in the next two weeks", I can do that. That's why you pay a monthly maintenance fee.

Q How long does it take?

A. The entire process can take anywhere between six weeks to six months. It depends on you. How fast can you implement the new processes? How quick can you train your staff?

Q Who is in charge of the process?

A. eLaunchers are. We have a dedicated project manager who runs the project and is in charge of the project management dashboard, making sure all of the pieces are taken care of.

You, your staff, and the other vendors report to the master dashboard and the master task list.

Q What do I have to do?

A. In a word, Lots. Putting an integrated automated sales and marketing system in place is a process that involves everyone's best efforts, you, your staff, and of course, us. But not to worry! We have procedures, systems, and applications in place that help you manage your workload. We're always there with you. We tell you exactly what needs to be done and put an expert beside you to complete the tasks.

You will either need to write or work with a writer that you hire. You will need to approve of the content and the strategy. You will also need to share your spirit that we then capture and share with the world. You will need to read what we give you and provide us with timely feedback.

We need to work as one cohesive force because you will need to put me in charge of your staff, who report to my project manager, my production manager, and my timeline when you buy my system.

Q Once this system is implemented, what work does my staff have to do?

A. We will discuss this in great detail during our first meeting. It depends on many factors, your staff, their technical aptitude, and what work the system assigns to people.

Most businesses follow this process:

- start with people
- give the person/people an apparatus
- assemble a workflow system
- as the business grows—add more people
- people bring their appliances and apparatuses
- data flows as an outgrowth of people, devices, and apparatuses

With my BRENT system, we start at the end, which puts people in control of the data. Here's how our process works:

- build a data system
- defer the apparatus to the data system
- defer people to the apparatus

Out of 465 things your marketing machine will do, 11-15 are assigned to people who have to do the work, such as learning and adopting the system, picking up the phone to call the prospect, and closing the deal. Your people are your single most significant asset.

Q Why should I go through this?

A. The core purpose of implementing an automated marketing system is to reduce dependency on people. If you do not have an automated system you are always exchanging physical work for hourly dollars. You are also relying on people to get things done. Depending on the reliability, health, and attitude of the people who do the work, it may or may not get done, and the consistency will vary.

You want to do this because you can only do so much on your own without burning out. With an automated sales system, the marketing machine can work 24/7 to generate leads that can be channeled into your sales funnel that converts into sales.

Q Do you do the printing?

A. Yes, we have a resident print production manager who will manage your printing, mailing, data processing, mail merge, and everything else. We do not own our print production facility. We work with a ½ dozen vendors we have built trusted relationships with over the years. We buy their services wholesale. For your production costs, you are paying for your project manager, the production manager's time, a small contribution to my overhead, and a small profit. The price is about 20-30% more than the market.

Our rule of thumb is that if a project is more extensive than $5000, it may make sense to ask one or more team members to coordinate and manage. If something goes wrong, we can take over the project and put it back on track.

Q How do you generate leads?

A. We generate leads through multiple methods:

- targeted email marketing
- external referral marketing (referral systems)
- online marketing
- social media
- targeted multi-step direct mail
- targeted every door direct mail
- internal client referral marketing
- external marketing
- free standing inserts

pre-and post-event marketing

Q What methods do you not use for sales and marketing?

A. The methods we do not use are:

- radio
- television
- public relations
- space/print advertising
- outdoor advertising
- vehicle wraps

Q Who develops the content?

A. To answer this question, you'll have to bear with me while I rant for a little while.

Effective sales content should capture your style and tone while increasing your brand awareness and powers of persuasion. There is an art and a science to making it sound like it comes from your heart. It should not be taken lightly, nor should it be outsourced to a staff member with some writing skills to save time or money.

If you insist on writing your content, learn from the masters; Dan Kennedy or Robert Cialdini. As I have. Dan Kennedy's books show you the formulas he's used to make millions of dollars from copywriting. Learning his techniques takes practice; developing consistent skills takes years.

If you don't have the time or feel confident yet in your copywriting ability, we can outsource it to a skilled copywriter. Or if you'd instead choose your own, we are happy to provide referrals.

Q What if I need videos?

A. Our consultation for determining what type of media you need is included in the fee. However, the video itself is an additional cost.

There are three types of videos:

1. PowerPoint slides with voice added to them

2. Animated videos like the ones you see on my website

3. Professional shot and edited videos

Regardless of which one you choose; you will need to follow the same six processes:

1. Define the purpose of your video

2. Create a video storyboard

3. Choreograph the video

4. Generate a draft of your video

5. Produce video scripts

6. Rehearse

Either we can outsource the videographer, or if you have someone you like to work with, by all means, hire them. If you need to fly out to a studio, we can arrange that for you too.

Q What are the most common mistakes people make when doing marketing on their own or hiring another firm?

A. Glad you asked! There are three areas I've identified in my 19+ years in the business:

1. Failing to plan. Creating a marketing plan is like writing an essay; you start with the end in mind or a goal and work backward. Planning extends to resources too, and you need to factor in the time, money, and resources required to deliver your project. You also need to set benchmarks or win conditions and, of course, the end goal.

2. Lack of clear expectations of needs, objectives, the results, and the reasons why these things are essential.

3. A lack of understanding of what constitutes successful implementation of a project and what constitutes failure of a project

Q There are lots of marketing companies, why should I choose you?

A. I don't claim to be the best at everything, but I do claim to be the best at understanding the correlation between data and money better than anybody else.

My goal is to make you two or three times as much money as you spent on my marketing consultation. Of course, like with everything else, I have a process for this.

But unlike everyone else, if you're not happy with the results, you can either have a do-over to see if we can do it better or have a 100% unconditional money-back guarantee.

Think about that.

Q What do I have to lose?

A. You've seen how I've worked with other businesses over 19 years to become a recognized expert.

You've heard how others have used BRENT to reap the benefits of an integrated, automated system.

Now it's time for a decision.

The way I see it, you have three options:

1. Do nothing and stay precisely where you are now.

2. If you aren't convinced that having an integrated, automated marketing and sales system is critical in today's business environment, you don't need BRENT's system.

3. But if you get that BRENT's system saves you time and money by automating your sales processes quickly and efficiently, you have two other options;

Do it yourself. Hire all the people and find all the processes to implement your automated sales and marketing system. If you want to do all the hard work, and take the hundreds of hours to accomplish this, more power to you.

Turn it over to me and let BRENT's system take the burden off your shoulders.

I will guide you through the process and work beside you at each step. I will show you how it integrates with your business to attract, convert, and retain customers.

Of these three options, the question that you will be asking yourself is, "How can I make this process easy for me and my business?"

I hope you're one of the people who take action when you see a good opportunity and are not the kind who sits on the fence and daydreams. Those who act are the ones who earn respect, trust, and business in their community. Because you've read this far, I believe you are one of the uncommon few who takes action.

Schedule a consultation session with me and get started on your path to profit with BRENT's automated system.

This call will help me understand your goals while we decide if working together is a good fit.

Thank you, and I look forward to speaking with you.

About
Parthiv Shah

Parthiv Shah is president and founder of eLaunchers.com and a serial entrepreneur who has started five small businesses, including one internet start-up. He works on hundreds of different business models every year and contributes to their revenue model. For over 19 years, the direct marketing industry and thousands of case studies have been the fabric of his life. He has mailed over a billion pieces of direct mail throughout his career and brought in over fifteen million dollars in business to his company.

Parthiv has a passion for small business with a soft corner in his heart for start-ups and not-yet-started start-ups and contributes pro bono marketing consulting work for fellow entrepreneurs. He enjoys helping small businesses develop their value proposition and identify market segments most suitable to their strengths.

He has been an implementation craftsman and data scientist all his life and started his career in direct mail marketing in 1989. Shah learned many tricks of the trade while working with direct mail guru Matt Perrone from 1989—2002 at J Perrone Company in Hingham, MA. In 1999, Parthiv started a dot-com company, failed to make it a success, and went back to work for J Perrone company.

In 2002, he left J Perrone again to start in Pembroke, MA. Listlaunchers began as a mailing list company helping printers, mail houses, direct marketers, fundraisers, and ad agencies with their list research & data acquisition needs. It evolved into a full service online/offline marketing campaign implementation firm specializing in automated marketing.

In 2006, Parthiv sold Listlaunchers to an Indian InfoTech company and started eLaunchers.com. eLaunchers.com is a turnkey sales lead generation and marketing company that helps small, and no-so-small businesses and organizations compete against rivals who have deep pockets and large marketing budgets. The elaunchers.com team has developed a data-driven direct marketing process that integrates e-mail, direct mail, and web.

Since Shah enjoys helping small businesses grow, eLaunchers.com is a **Done For You** Implementation company helping small to mid-sized businesses experience a transformational marketing makeover within 48 hours to fifteen days. The entire game plays on Hubspot, WordPress, Keap, membership sites, SQL tables, PURL engine, and custom object-oriented programming.

Elaunchers.com has a global workforce with marketing and data experts in America, and API developers., Mobile App developers, and object-oriented programmers, and Web/CRM implementation specialists in other countries.

Parthiv has also taught marketing and e-business to MBA students at the University of Phoenix MBA School of Business.

Originally from India, he immigrated to the USA in 1990 and lived with his family in Randolph, Massachusetts, a little south of Boston.

He resided in Boyds, Maryland, since 2014 when eLaunchers. com purchased the office space in Germantown, which is home to eLaunchers.com's corporate headquarters.

Parthiv has a bachelor's degree in sociology from Gujarat State University and an MBA in marketing from Bentley College.

Book bonus: To read additional books by Parthiv Shah's or to request an invitation to join his book club, please go to https://elaunchers.com/books.

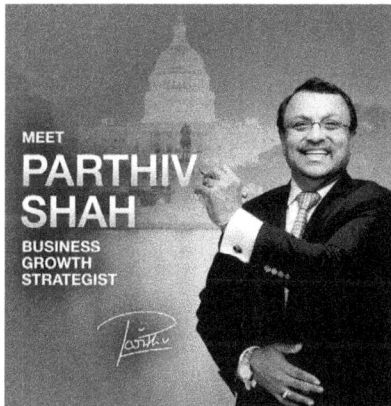

Connect with Parthiv:

Got questions? Want to talk to Parthiv? You can ask him questions at www.askparthiv.com or schedule a call with him at www.meetparthiv.com

COULD I ASK YOU A SMALL FAVOR?

Thank you for reading my BRENT NEVER FORGETS book! I know if you follow what I've written, you'll be well on your way to automating your sales and marketing systems.

I have a tiny favor to ask. Would you be willing to leave a candid review for this book on Amazon?

Reviews are the best way to help other business owners and entrepreneurs solve problems by buying this book. I read all my reviews for helpful comments.

If you have questions not addressed in my book, or you'd just like to share your feedback about my book, send me an email at pshah@elaunchers.com. I'd really love to hear from you!

www.ingramcontent.com/pod-product-compliance
Lightning Source LLC
Chambersburg PA
CBHW071552200326
41519CB00021BB/6717